The Bible
A Beginner's Guide

"With her characteristic clarity and ability to make biblical scholarship accessible to all, Paula Gooder here provides a valuable overview of key issues that affect how one should approach the Bible."

Christine Joynes – Director, Centre for Reception History of the Bible, University of Oxford, UK

"Gooder is a rare combination of distinguished scholar and superb communicator. Here, she combines these gifts to outstanding effect. Her learning is worn very lightly indeed. Highly recommended."

Paul Joyce – Samuel Davidson Professor of Old Testament/ Hebrew Bible, King's College London, UK

"In a clear, thoughtful and accessible way, this book succeeds in introducing the interested reader to the many complexities connected with the Bible, its history, reception and interpretation, from antiquity to the present day."

James Carleton Paget – Senior Lecturer in New Testament Studies, University of Cambridge, UK

"A wonderful balance. Very engaging and remarkably complete."

Roy Heller – Associate Professor of Old Testament, Perkins School of Theology at the Southern Methodist University, USA

ONEWORLD BEGINNER'S GUIDES combine an original, inventive, and engaging approach with expert analysis on subjects ranging from art and history to religion and politics, and everything in between. Innovative and affordable, books in the series are perfect for anyone curious about the way the world works and the big ideas of our time.

The Bible
A Beginner's Guide

Paula Gooder

ONEWORLD

A Oneworld Book

Published by Oneworld Publications 2013

ISBN 978-1-85168-990-3
ISBN (ebook) 978-1-78074-239-7

Typeset by Cenveo, India
Printed and bound in Great Britain by
TJ International Ltd, Cornwall

Oneworld Publications
10 Bloomsbury Street
London WC1B 3SR
UK

Stay up to date with the latest books,
special offers, and exclusive content from
Oneworld with our monthly newsletter

Sign up on our website
www.oneworld-publications.com

For my big sister,
Rachel Martin

Contents

List of maps and illustrations

Introduction

The Bible is the bestselling book of all times. It is estimated that the Bible has sold more than 2.5 billion copies (or in the region of six billion copies if you count the ones that have been given away) and that around 100 million copies are sold each year. People read the Bible for all sorts of reasons. Some read it to enrich and enhance their faith; others read it from the perspective of no faith, curious to discover what it might have to say. Some read for help with moral guidance; others read it to help them understand biblical allusions in literature or film. Some approach it with enthusiasm; others with dread. Some have read it – or parts of it – many times before; others come to it for the first time.

Whoever they are and whatever their purpose in reading the Bible, most need some assistance in reading the Bible. At somewhere between 1500 and 2000 pages (depending on the edition), the Bible is to say the least daunting … and that is even before opening it. Only the most determined and focused of readers can hope to begin to make any sense of the Bible without some kind of help along the way. This book seeks to offer this kind of help, to set up signposts, to answer key questions and to map territory so that you can begin to recognize the landmarks and key features of the text and its importance throughout history. This is not a 'how to' guide (there are many of those on the market already); instead it is a book *about* the Bible, what's in it, how it got to be like it is today and what impact it has made on the world in which we live. It won't tell you everything you need to know but it will give you a flavour of some of the things you might need to know if you are going to get to grips with it.

The Bible all around you

The Bible is less well known today than fifty years ago but nevertheless a large number of references to it remain in our contemporary culture, even though many people have lost the awareness that they are there. Go into any toy store and one of the major themes of toys for babies that you can find is Noah's ark. When my children were tiny they had a Noah's ark play mat, numerous books on Noah and his ark and even a squishy Noah's ark which contained fabric lions, bears, elephants and other animals.

Another way in which the Bible influences our modern culture is through words or phrases from the Bible which are now used to name certain organizations. Probably the best-known example of this is 'Samaritans', an organization which aims to offer help to people in need of emotional support. Its name comes, not from the religious group who lived in an area known as Samaria in the Holy Land at the time of Jesus (and who continue to live there today though in very small numbers), but from the story in the New Testament often called the Good Samaritan in which an unnamed Samaritan stopped to help a Jew in need despite neither knowing him nor having anything in common.

Probably the greatest influence, though, of the Bible on our modern world is in the words and phrases which we still use and which are drawn directly from the Bible: phrases like 'a baptism of fire' (Matthew 3.11); 'a breath of life' (Genesis 2.7); 'an eye for an eye and a tooth for a tooth' (Exodus 21.24 and elsewhere); 'the fat of the land' (Genesis 45.18); 'the letter of the law' (2 Corinthians 3.6); 'there is nothing new under the sun' (Ecclesiastes 1.9); 'pride goes before a fall' (Proverbs 16.18); 'set your teeth on edge' and 'sour grapes' (Jeremiah 31.30); 'sufficient unto the day' (Matthew 6.34). The list could go on and on but the point is easily made. Our language is deeply and profoundly shaped by the Bible (and in particular by the King James translation of the Bible).

If we were to attempt to remove the Bible from every part of our modern world we would lose huge numbers of poems, plays and novels (including those by Shakespeare, Wordsworth and Tennyson), many, many works of art, music and film, a large number of sayings and quite a number of children's toys too! The point is that whether we are aware of it or not the Bible is all around us and cannot be removed from our modern culture very easily.

Whose Bible is it anyway?

The fact that the Bible is thoroughly embedded in our culture raises the question of whose Bible is it? In many world religions which have sacred texts, this would be an easy question to answer, since sacred texts are often only sacred to one religion. The Bible is more complex than that however. It contains the sacred texts of both Judaism and Christianity but is also regarded by Islam as containing true revelation, albeit a revelation that has been corrupted by human hands. Within Islam, the Torah (the first five books of the Bible), for example, is regarded as being the Word of God but that various additions have been made to it over time that have corrupted it. In the same way, the Qur'an refers to the gospel that was revealed to Jesus Christ as a divinely revealed book, but believes that the Gospels of Matthew, Mark, Luke and John are human corruptions of that original gospel.

Within Judaism and Christianity the Bible is more than a humanly corrupted Word of God: it is sacred Scripture. Within Judaism, what is called by Christians the Old Testament is varyingly called the Hebrew Bible, the Hebrew Scriptures or Tanakh and comprises the Jewish Scriptures. Within Judaism, the Torah holds a particular place in terms of Scripture and is viewed as containing part of what was revealed to Moses on Mount Sinai (the other part is known as Oral Law or Halakhah which is believed to have been handed down from the time of Moses).

The addition of what Christians call the New Testament to the Hebrew Scriptures (called by Christians the Old Testament) makes a total collection of the sixty-six books which make up the Christian Bible. For Christians, the Bible contains the Word of God which can be encountered when the Scriptures are read and interpreted.

Although the Bible is supremely important for both Judaism and Christianity, that is not the sole extent of its influence. The domination of Christianity in the West for many centuries also means that the Bible extends a powerful influence into many Western societies. There is an argument to be made for saying that as well as belonging to two major world religions and being respected by a third, the Bible also belongs to all those societies that have been deeply shaped by it at some point in their history (though whether they would, today, want to acknowledge such an ownership is another matter altogether).

What this illustrates, though, is that the influence of the Bible stretches far beyond the boundaries of the communities that call it sacred. The Bible is deeply embedded in the society in which we live and as such needs to be explored, at least in part, if we are to have any hope of understanding why our society functions as it does.

For Jews and Christians, the Bible remains a deeply relevant text which continues to shape who they are and what they do. For others, while it is much less obviously relevant day to day, it maintains a continued influence in terms of culture and language. For both sets of people, it is worth getting to know the Bible better and to see the ways in which the Bible has been important for so long and for so many people.

An outline of the *Beginner's Guide to the Bible*

One of the great challenges of writing a book such as this is not so much finding something to say as working out what not to say. Almost by definition a beginner's guide to a subject as large as this one will involve missing out more than is put in. The question then becomes how to decide what to miss out. After a great deal of thought I decided to shape the book around the questions that I am most often asked about the Bible. These are:

- What happened when? (History)
- What kind of a book is it? (Genre)
- Why these books and not others? (Canon)
- Which is the best translation? (Translation)
- Why does the Bible need interpretation? (Interpretation)

The final chapter, chapter 6 ('Legacy'), is the only chapter that does not emerge out of questions that I am often asked. I have included it in this book, however, because the question of the impact that the Bible has had on our culture is such an important one, even though we are often so familiar with certain themes that we overlook that they came originally from the Bible.

The book is very much an introduction and if you find that you would like to explore any of the areas in the book in more detail then, at the end of the book, you will find a range of suggestions for further reading, organised by chapter, so that you can follow ideas up more fully.

The overall picture you get from looking at the different questions raised in the chapters of this book is a picture of the Bible that is far more important and influential even than a total of six billion printed texts suggests. It is a book with roots that stretch far back in history not just hundreds but thousands of years, whose contents continue to shape the societies in which we live (even if we are less aware of this now than we used to be) and whose long journey from ancient Hebrew and Greek text to modern English translation has changed the world we inhabit along the way.

1

History

Introduction

One of the great challenges that faces anyone who wants to read even a bit of the Bible is that the biblical writers assume that their readers know the major historical events that lie behind the text. If you don't you can be confused about what is really going on. To make it even more complicated the Bible isn't even in chronological order. So although parts of it seem to follow on one from the other, other parts dot around all over the place. Take the Minor Prophets, for example. The first four Minor Prophets are Hosea, Joel, Amos and Obadiah. Hosea is thought to have written into the eighth century BC, whereas Joel is thought to be addressing an audience maybe 200 years later in the sixth century BC. Amos is back in the eighth century and Obadiah could fall either in the ninth century BC or the seventh century. Unless you have some kind of framework that helps you to understand what happened when, you can very quickly become hopelessly lost in the maze of kings of Israel and Judah; the difference between Syria and Assyria; the connection between the Babylonians and the Persians and so on.

In order to keep up with when and where things happened, it helps to have a rough sketch in your mind of the history of Israel until 70 AD. This chapter seeks to take a swift journey through the history of the Bible in order to give a framework onto which you can hang some of the key events of the Bible and see how they all fit together. It is far from exhaustive and seeks just to give an outline, nothing more.

It is also worth noting at this point that when a book is set is not necessarily when it is written. Then as now, people wrote history in which they describe events that took place sometimes hundreds of years before.

The beginning

Reading the Bible may be one of those occasions where the very beginning is not a good place to start, or at least not when you are interested in the question of history. In fact, the question of when history begins in the Bible may well have caused more conflict than any other subject. The obvious answer to the question of when history begins is when time begins, and yet giving this answer throws up all sorts of questions which are not easy to answer. Creationism – the belief that the world was created as reported in Genesis – is most often discussed these days in terms of science and its relationship to evolution, but it is also a belief about history. Many Creationists believe that chapters 1–2 of Genesis are historical accounts about the origin of the world. For them, history begins with Adam and Eve.

Of course, not everyone holds this view. Indeed there are a good number of scholars today who might be placed at the other end of the spectrum from Creationists on this issue. These scholars argue that the majority of the Bible originates a long, long time after it is set and that much of it comes from the time of the Persian and Hellenistic empires (i.e. the sixth century BC onwards). For them the vast majority of the history of the Bible is unreliable, written later by people who were attempting to re-invent their history once they came to the land from Babylon. As a result they don't just doubt the historicity of Adam and Eve but of Moses, Joshua, David and Isaiah too.

There are of course many positions about the history of the Bible that people can hold between these two extremes. Some argue that while Adam and Eve may not be historical, Abraham was. Others think that the accounts about Abraham are too vague and personal to be history and so trace history from

King David onwards, or from the time of the eighth century when prophets like Amos and Hosea are said to have lived. The question of history in the Bible is complex and controversial and there are no easy answers as to how to proceed. The debate about the historicity of the Bible rages on between scholars and each reader will need to form their own view about when they think the Bible moves from being 'story' to 'history'. Some will think history begins with Genesis 1; others with Abraham or Moses; others with David and Solomon; and others still with Ezra and Nehemiah.

One of the real problems we face is that we simply do not have the kind of evidence we might need in order to be confident about what happened when. For that we would need a wide variety of texts (not just biblical ones) which all tallied in terms of dates and which also tallied with ample archaeological findings. Instead what we have is a majority of evidence from just one source, the Bible, a few scattered external sources which sometime tally with the Bible and sometimes don't and archaeological findings which are hard to tie up with the biblical narrative. None of this means that the Bible is necessarily historically inaccurate; simply that it is hard to demonstrate the history to the extent that we might want to.

The debate about historicity is really irresolvable. The kind of evidence that we would need to demonstrate the historicity of these texts beyond a shadow of a doubt almost certainly doesn't exist. It might be possible to prove parts of the narrative to the satisfaction of some people but it is impossible to prove all of the narrative to the satisfaction of everyone. The swift re-telling of history in the pages that follow has no time to stop and explore the controversial questions about what might or might not have happened. Instead it is just trying to put the key events in order with some possible dates alongside to give a rough map of how the different events relate to each other.

The account of history that follows begins with the call of Abraham in Genesis 12, because with him the story of a people chosen by God for a special relationship with God begins. Chapters 1–11 of Genesis are different kinds of account, with talking snakes, angels with fiery swords, sons of God who have sexual relationships with human women, and towers that their builders believe will reach to heaven. Although there are sporadic references to these events throughout the rest of the Old Testament (and indeed the New Testament too), the concentration of them here (together with the subject matter of creation and the fall) suggests that Genesis 1–11 is a different kind of narrative. Indeed many scholars call these chapters primeval history to indicate that they have a different kind of content and message to what follows them. The story of Abraham is where the 'story' of God's people begins – it is up to you to decide whether you think this is the story of God's people or the history of God's people.

In each section of the history below, I have provided a rough date for the characters that feature in the relevant part of the Bible. This is meant to give you a very approximate idea of when these events might have taken place. The aim of the telling of the history below is to give an outline of the key events: more of a bird's eye view than a detailed blow-by-blow examination of the stories, their authorship, and any historical problem that you might encounter while reading them.

God's promise to Abraham

ROUGH POSSIBLE HISTORICAL DATE: c.1800 BC (middle to late Bronze Age)

RECORDED IN Genesis 12–50

KEY CHARACTERS: Abraham and Sarah, Jacob, Leah and Rachel, Joseph's twelve sons

OUTLINE OF EVENTS: God promised Abraham that he would give him descendants and a land to live in. At first he had no children; then once he had many descendants, his family left the land of Canaan and moved to Egypt.

The story of the people of God starts with Abram (who was later renamed Abraham by God) since with him begins the story of a particular relationship between God and a specific family. The stories in this part of Genesis are often called the Patriarchal Narratives, and refer to the key figures of Abraham, Isaac and Jacob (and their wives) who ruled over the clan which descended from Abraham.

The narratives told are uneven in terms of detail. There are times, like the time when Abraham and Sarah are waiting for a child, when quite precise detail is given; whereas at other times, like much of Isaac's life, vast tracts of time are skipped over in a very cursory manner. The account gives the impression of being a little like a family photo album which misses out the less important moments in the family's life and spends much longer on key moments which are important to the family's story of who they are and what has made them who they are. So there are years where there is little entered in the 'album' and then pages and pages of one or two key events.

The key focus of this part of the story is God's promise to Abraham which is summarized in Genesis 12.1–2:

> Now the Lord said to Abram, 'Go from your country and your kindred and your father's house to the land that I will show you. I will make of you a great nation, and I will bless you, and make your name great, so that you will be a blessing.'

There are three key parts to the promise:

- that God will provide Abraham with descendants ('I will make of you a great nation');
- that God will give Abraham's descendants land in which to live ('Go from your country and your kindred and your father's house to the land that I will show you');
- that God will maintain a special relationship with Abraham and his descendants ('I will bless you, and make your name great, so that you will be a blessing').

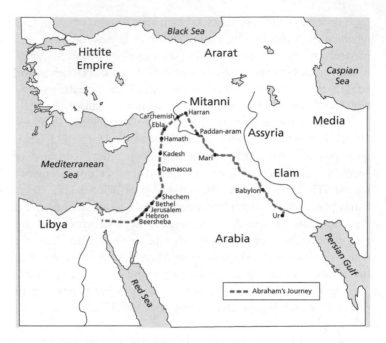

Figure 1 Abraham's journey from Ur to Canaan

Genesis 12–50 is, roughly speaking, centred around this promise and the various crises that emerge when it looks as though one or another of these promises might not be fulfilled.

The first half of this story about the Patriarchs focuses on the question of whether Abraham will ever become the father of a great nation. For most of the story about Abraham, Abraham and Sarah have no children of their own which makes the promise of being the father of a great nation unlikely in the extreme. Even once Sarah gave birth to a much-longed-for son (Genesis 21.3), the question about whether Abraham will be the father of a great nation does not resolve for a long time, not least because Abraham is then commanded by God to kill Isaac (Genesis 22.2).

The second half of the story switches attention to the land (Genesis 25–50). Soon Abraham had many descendants, through his grandson Jacob who had twelve sons, but these descendants moved away from Canaan to Egypt. This then threw up the question of whether the great nation whose father was Abraham would in fact ever live in the land that God had promised them. The book of Genesis ends on a knife edge, with God's promise to Abraham still in crisis. Abraham now had many, many descendants but these now numerous descendants lived far away from Canaan in Egypt where they had gone to stay with Joseph, Jacob's son, to avoid a famine in Canaan.

THE HISTORICAL ABRAHAM?

The complexities and problems of demonstrating the historicity of the Bible are well illustrated with the character of Abraham. Over the years many people have argued vociferously for Abraham's historicity, while others with the same evidence have argued just as vehemently against it.

The problem is that the kind of evidence we would need to prove Abraham's existence beyond any shadow of a doubt almost certainly could not exist. Abraham was semi-nomadic and is said to have travelled over hundreds of miles during his lifetime. For much of this time he did not live in cities, but in a small tented community. The chance of digging up evidence of his existence is slim in the extreme, and even if archaeological evidence could be discovered it would be very hard to tie it to the Abraham of the Bible.

The best we can hope for is to argue that someone like Abraham could have existed in the relevant timeframe. Here we can find evidence but none of it very strong. One of the odd features of the Abraham narrative is that twice Abraham passed his wife off as his sister (and following that Isaac did it once too).

There is evidence that this was a Hurrian custom (the Hurrians were an ancient people who lived in the region of Ur around the time that Abraham might also have lived there). Some scholars have also argued that names like Abraham or Jacob were in use in this region in the second millennium BC (i.e. the possible date for Abraham). Other pieces of evidence can be put forward but all are equally flimsy.

What this illustrates is that the existence of Abraham can neither be proved nor disproved. As a result we must treat these stories for they are – ancient tales of family events – more important for what they tell us about the people than for historical evidence.

Leaving Egypt and settling in the land

ROUGH POSSIBLE HISTORICAL DATE: c.1300 BC (late Bronze Age to Iron Age 1)

RECORDED IN Exodus, Numbers, Deuteronomy, Joshua, Judges, 1 Samuel 1–8

KEY CHARACTERS: Moses, Joshua, Deborah, Gideon, Samson, Samuel

OUTLINE OF EVENTS: Abraham's descendants were numerous but enslaved in Egypt. Moses led them out of slavery, through the desert and eventually, under Joshua, they settled in Canaan. At this point they were twelve warring tribes in need of a leader.

The next phase of the history opens in Egypt many years after the death of Joseph in what is probably the late Bronze Age. Here the nature of the story has changed. The narrative is no longer concerned with a particular family but with a whole, now numerous, group of people who are descendants of Abraham. It focuses now on the question of whether this people will be able to make their way to the land of Canaan which God had promised to them via Abraham years before.

The story picks up again in Egypt where Joseph's descendants have stopped being honoured guests of the Pharaoh and have become instead slaves of an oppressive nation. The first half of the book of Exodus recounts Moses' struggle with Pharaoh in his attempt to persuade him to free the people of God and eventual flight from Egypt across the Red Sea into the Sinai Peninsula.

The next forty years were spent, according to the book of Numbers (Numbers 14.33–34), in the Sinai Peninsula (a time often called the Wilderness Wanderings) until the generation who had left Egypt with Moses had died and the new generation were ready to enter the Promised Land. The biblical accounts attribute this period of wandering to the fact that those who left Egypt sinned and were not ready to enter the land that God had promised them. Deuteronomy records that Moses also died (Deuteronomy 34.5) and that he was succeeded as leader by Joshua who then led the people into Canaan.

One of the challenges of the accounts at this point is that Joshua and Judges appear to tell a very different story. The book of Joshua seems to recount a simple invasion and conquering of the land of Canaan; whereas the book of Judges tells a much more involved narrative of continual struggle with the inhabitants of the land, some of whom they killed and some of whom they lived alongside. For example:

> Joshua 11.23: So Joshua took the whole land, according to all that the LORD had spoken to Moses; and Joshua gave it for an inheritance to Israel according to their tribal allotments. And the land had rest from war.

and:

> Judges 15.63: But the people of Judah could not drive out the
> Jebusites, the inhabitants of Jerusalem; so the Jebusites live with
> the people of Judah in Jerusalem to this day.

The two accounts represent two different ways of viewing this
part of the narrative: one easily successful; one more drawn out
and complex.

The period depicted by the book of Judges is the period after
God's people settled in the land but before they had a king. It is
not an easy period to grasp. The book of Judges deliberately tells
a chaotic, confusing story of twelve tribes who were trying to
settle in a land where others already dwelt. The story speaks of
conflicts not only with the people who already lived in the land
of Canaan but between the different tribes of the people of God.
This period reflects a time in which it is almost impossible to talk
about a 'nation' or a 'people'; instead it is a time in which the
tribes were far from unified and were led for short periods of
time by successive, charismatic leaders.

The stories are scattered, lacking in cohesion and, although
interesting on their own, hard to fit together. The book of 1
Samuel deliberately links its opening to the end of this period. The
period of the Judges is chaotic and not cohesive. 1 Samuel begins
here as a way of illustrating how great a change is about to take
place. The next phase of the story is a phase marked by increasing
cohesion (at least for a while) and the story tries to illustrate not
only what changes but why it was so important that it did change.

Finding a king and unity

ROUGH POSSIBLE HISTORICAL DATE: c.1020 to c.922 BC (Iron
Age II)

RECORDED IN 1 and 2 Samuel, 1 Kings 1–12, and 1 Chronicles and 2 Chronicles 1–9

KEY CHARACTERS: Samuel, Saul, David, Solomon, Rehoboam

OUTLINE OF EVENTS: Samuel anointed a leader, Saul, for the people, but he was soon replaced by David. David, an astute religious and political leader, united the tribes and set up a capital in Jerusalem. However, there were cracks in the unity even then. These cracks split open during Solomon's reign, and when his son, Rehoboam, became king, Israel split into two.

Following the chaos of the period of the Judges, the story of 1 Samuel sees the account become more focused again. In Judges, the story of God's people was a story of twelve separate tribes. From Saul onwards the focus moved once more into telling a single story about the people of God (though at times this story is told from different perspectives).

The opening chapters of 1 Samuel set up a scene which speaks of the dire need that the people had for a leader, as even worship of God had become corrupt, with the family of the priest taking more than their share of the food that was sacrificed. One of the intriguing features of this part of the story is that there are two distinct voices speaking in the text – one thinks that the only solution for Israel is to have a king (1 Samuel 9.1–10, 11.1–15) and the other that having a king would be disastrous (8.1–22, 10.17–27, 12.1–25). This can be confusing as you read through the text and these two voices, though less clear once they have a permanent king, still speak from time to time as you read on. These two voices reflect the different opinions of kingship in Israel. For some the king was God's anointed leader who would save the people from oppression; for others he was the very reason they were oppressed in the first place.

The first king of God's people was Saul, who was anointed by the prophet Samuel while Saul searched for his father's lost donkeys (1 Samuel 9) and/or was elected by popular acclaim (1 Samuel 10.17–27). Although he is said to have been anointed as 'king' he is more often referred to just as a 'leader'. This means he often has more in common with leaders like Gideon or Deborah than with David and Solomon who follow him as king and indeed this is reinforced by the fact that his influence stretches over a few central tribes but not the whole of the twelve tribes of Israel.

Saul's reign was relatively short-lived but it is hard to tell precisely why. 1 Samuel attributes it to his disobedience to a command of God (1 Samuel 13.13–14) but also hints at mental illness in the king with references to an evil spirit descending on him (1 Samuel 16.23). Whatever the reason, Samuel soon anointed David as king to succeed Saul (1 Samuel 16.13) and for the next few years David was at war with Saul, until he was eventually successful and Saul was killed in battle (1 Samuel 31).

To start with David was crowned king in Hebron (2 Samuel 2.1–3) and ruled primarily over the southern tribes of Israel. It was only later that he moved his capital to Jerusalem (2 Samuel 5.6). The genius of the move to Jerusalem is clear. Even at this point there was considerable enmity between the ten northern tribes and two southern tribes. Jerusalem lay almost directly in the middle of their two regions and was a Jebusite city (i.e. it belonged neither to the tribes of the north nor to the tribes of the south). It therefore provided a central neutral territory in which David could consolidate his rule. The rest of the reign of David saw a period of fast expansion of territory and of reputation; a period in which, probably for the first time, we can begin to talk of Israel and not just of the twelve tribes of the people of God.

It is worth noting, though, that even in David's reign there were cracks which suggest that the unity of the tribes was not as firm as you might otherwise think. There were a number of rebellions during David's reign. In one of them, David's son

Absalom persuaded the southern tribes around Hebron to rebel against David and in another someone from the north, Sheba, son of Bichri, urged schism. These cracks were never fully healed and in fact became even wider during the otherwise successful reign of David's son Solomon.

Solomon's reign was one characterized by wealth, a strong building programme and outward success. One of his greatest achievements was the building of the temple. Until this point the Ark of the Covenant, which housed the commandments given by God to Moses on Mount Sinai and which was believed to be the place on which God's presence would descend when God came down to earth, had been housed in a tent or Tabernacle. David himself had wanted to build a permanent structure in which the people could worship God but was forbidden by God from doing so. Solomon, however, was allowed to build the temple and did so to great acclaim. The temple, the growing wealth of the kingdom, and his international renown (Solomon is said to have been visited by the Queen of Sheba because she had heard of his reputation, 1 Kings 10.1) all led to Solomon's reign being viewed as a huge success. But behind this glamorous story of wealth, huge numbers of women (Solomon is said to have had at least seven hundred wives and three hundred concubines), and achievement is the less glamorous underbelly of Solomon's reign which built success on the oppression of his own people and seems to have led to the kingdom splitting apart after his death.

After Solomon's death, the northern tribes came to visit Rehoboam, Solomon's son, to beg him to be more lenient towards them than his father had been. Rehoboam refused and promised instead to be even harsher towards them. This caused a large-scale revolt among the ten northern tribes which rebelled against Rehoboam and the two southern tribes. As a result David's kingdom split apart and became two nations: Israel in the north (made up of the ten northern tribes) and Judah in the south (made up of the two southern tribes).

The short-lived unity of the people of God was at an end. From this moment onwards the north and the south had separate kings, separate worship centres, and for the most part a separate history.

It is worth noting that the naming of these two kingdoms can be problematic and confusing, not least because the nations are not always called by the same name. The Northern Kingdom is, among other things, sometimes called Ephraim and sometimes Israel. Unfortunately the Southern Kingdom is also sometimes called Israel and sometimes Judah.

An independent Northern Kingdom

ROUGH HISTORICAL DATE: c.922 to 735 BC

RECORDED IN 1 Kings 11–2 Kings 13, Amos, Hosea

KEY CHARACTERS: Rehoboam, Jeroboam, Omri, Ahab and Jezebel, Elijah and Elisha

OUTLINE OF EVENTS: Jeroboam led a successful revolt against Rehoboam, Solomon's son, and by doing so established the independence of the Northern Kingdom. Israel, the Northern Kingdom, was ruled by a succession of charismatic leaders who were replaced in a series of coups.

The next phase of history requires two parallel sections, one for the Northern Kingdom (Israel) and one for the Southern Kingdom (Judah), since they are now separate nations. Reading the accounts in 1 and 2 Kings is particularly confusing since the account flicks from one to the other and back again. To make it even more complex the kings from the North and South have very similar sounding names so it is all too easy to lose where you are in the narrative.

Figure 2 The two kingdoms of Israel and Judah

Jeroboam led the revolt against Rehoboam. 1 Kings 11.28 states that he was in charge of the forced labour that Solomon had established to give him sufficient builders to complete his massive building programme. Fed up with the way that they were treated, the ten northern tribes declared their independence under Jeroboam from the house of David (1 Kings 12.16) and became a separate nation. One of the striking things about the Northern Kingdom is that unlike the Southern Kingdom they never founded a long-term royal dynasty. Their southern neighbours stayed with King David's descendants as kings but in the north no real alternative dynasty ever emerged. In fact the Northern Kingdom seemed to go back to the time of the Judges and of Saul. In this period, leadership emerged with charismatic, military figures rather than with royal dynasties.

Whether intentionally or not, the kings of the Northern Kingdom seem to have been selected (and discarded) in the way that Saul was. In other words, they were chosen because of their charismatic personality or military prowess (or both) and then they – or their descendants – were removed from power when someone else came along. Even a brief reading of 1 and 2 Kings reveals the bumpy legacy of the Northern Kingdom. Take for example Nadab the son of Jeroboam. When Jeroboam died he established his son, Nadab, on the throne (1 Kings 15.25). Nadab lasted for two years before being deposed by Baasha son of Ahijah. When Baasha died he was replaced by his son, Elah. Elah lasted two years before being deposed by Zimri (1 Kings 16), and so the story rolled on.

The story of the Northern Kingdom is one of an unhappy series of coups and counter-coups. Only one dynasty had any semblance of success in the two hundred years of Israel's history. This is the dynasty of Omri, who was a powerful commander of the army (1 Kings 16.16) and who established the capital at Samaria (1 Kings 16.24). Although the dynasty only lasted for three kings, these three kings ruled for around thirty years. In Israel's troubled history this gave them a much needed period of stability. The dynasty was also of note because of Omri's son: Ahab. Ahab is an infamous character in 1 Kings not least because he was married to Jezebel (who has gone down in popular imagination, probably unfairly, as one of the most wicked women of the Bible). Ahab and Jezebel were opposed vehemently by the prophet Elijah. In many ways Ahab was no more or less wicked than any king before or after him, but he did symbolize the problems faced by both kingdoms in this period.

Israel and Judah were very small nations and so needed to make alliances with their neighbours in order to survive. This they did through marriage. Jezebel, for example, was the daughter of the King of Sidon, to the north of Israel. The problem was that Jezebel, unsurprisingly, brought her own religion with her – the worship of Baal. The great narrative of conflict between Elijah and Jezebel is a narrative of Jezebel's attempt to instil her own religion in the land and Elijah's determined efforts to oppose this. The conflict that ensued included, for example, the standoff between Elijah and Jezebel's prophets of Baal on Mount Carmel. So important was this conflict that a major part of late 1 Kings and early 2 Kings (1 Kings 17–2 Kings 13, often called the Elijah and Elisha cycle) focuses not on the kings, as it has done for most of the narrative, but on Elijah and Elisha's attempts to combat the power of Omri's dynasty. Following Omri's dynasty, however, the narrative – and the system of coups – returned to normal, as does the account which switches its attention back to the kings and their deeds once more.

One of the noticeable features of the account of Israel's history at this point is the rise and importance of key prophetic figures like Elijah and Elisha who began to critique the king and what he did. This period sees the rise of other prophets – in the north these included Hosea and Amos – prophets who not only criticized the king but the whole of the Northern Kingdom for the way in which they failed to live up to what God expected of them. The prophets became a crucial voice in the life and history of both Northern and Southern Kingdoms, critiquing the nations from inside and attempting to get them to live more faithfully.

During this period, something else was happening outside the land of Israel and Judah which would, in time, have catastrophic consequences for one of the two kingdoms. Assyria

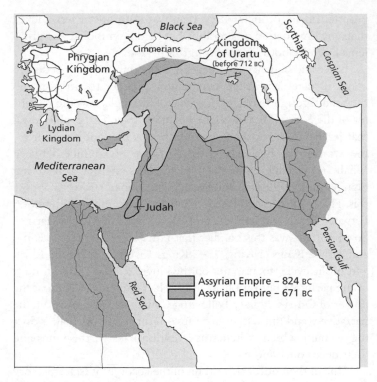

Figure 3 The Assyrian Empire

(much of whose territory overlaps with modern Iraq) had a long and glorious history which stretched back possibly as far as the third millennium BC. For most of its history, though it was wealthy and powerful, it had little impact on the story we are tracing here but, in the ninth century BC, the Neo-Assyrian Empire began to expand across the ancient Near East and under Shalmaneser III (c.858–24 BC) conquered Israel, Judah, and their neighbours, forcing them to pay tribute to the Assyrians.

An independent Southern Kingdom

ROUGH HISTORICAL DATE: c.922 to c.735 BC

RECORDED IN 1 Kings 11–16, 2 Kings 13–15, 2 Chronicles 10–27

KEY CHARACTERS: Rehoboam, Asa, Athaliah

OUTLINE OF EVENTS: Following the split of the Northern and Southern Kingdoms, the Southern Kingdom continued to be ruled by the Davidic dynasty. They were much weakened by the invasion early on of the Egyptian empire but had a more stable history than their neighbours in the north.

There are a few things worth noting about the biblical sources at this point. The first is that the books of Chronicles are, for the most part, a repetition of the details of 1 and 2 Kings but with a particular focus on the Southern Kingdom.

The Southern Kingdom was what was left once the Northern Kingdom had turned its back on Rehoboam. The two remaining tribes, Benjamin and Judah, made up the much less populous and much less wealthy Southern Kingdom of Judah. It may seem odd that Rehoboam didn't immediately launch a counter attack on Jeroboam, since Jerusalem had a superior infrastructure and, of course, the symbolic pull of Solomon's temple. In reality the kings of Judah did spend the next sixty years or so at war with their neighbours in the north, but soon after Jeroboam's rebellion they were invaded by Shishaq, a Pharaoh in Egypt. Rehoboam avoided destruction by giving Shishaq the temple treasure (some wonder whether the Ark of the Covenant was also handed over at this point) and as a result Judah was forced to pay tribute to Egypt. As a result, Judah simply did not have the resources to mount a successful campaign against Israel.

One of the unsung heroes of this era was Asa, grandson of Rehoboam, who, while the Northern Kingdom was hit by one rebellion after another, maintained peace in Judah for thirty-five years, despite a running battle with Baasha, king of Israel (who had killed Nadab, son of Jeroboam, in order to become king). Towards the end of Asa's reign, Baasha attempted to cut Judah off and by doing so to gain control over it. Asa bought the support of Ben-hadad, king of Syria, with the temple treasure. Ben-hadad then broke his alliance with the Northern Kingdom of Israel and threatened them to such an extent that Baasha ended his attempt to blockade Judah (see 2 Chronicles 16.1–14).

One additional intriguing bit of history from this era was the very brief period when Israel and Judah were ruled by people from the same family. Exactly what happened in this period is made doubly confusing by the fact that some of the kings of Israel and Judah have the same name. The infamous King Ahab was succeeded first by his son Ahaziah, and then by another son (brother of Ahaziah) called Joram (or sometimes Jehoram). Ahab also had a daughter called Athaliah and she was married to another Jehoram who was king of Judah. Their son was also called Ahaziah and he ruled after his father Jehoram. After the death of Ahaziah, king of Judah, Athaliah, who was very ambitious and ruthless, ruled over Judah for six years, until deposed by a long-lost (male) relative of Jehoram, king of Judah. This is fascinating because for a short period Judah, the great enemy of the Northern Kingdom, was ruled not only by a woman but by the daughter of the much hated Ahab.

The fall of Israel

ROUGH HISTORICAL DATE: c.735 to c.722 BC

RECORDED IN 2 Kings 15–18.10, Isaiah 7.1–9, 2 Chronicles 27–8

KEY CHARACTERS: Ahaz (king of Judah), Isaiah (prophet), Rezin (king of Syria), Pekah (king of Israel), Tiglath-Pileser III, Shalmaneser V and Sargon II (kings of Assyria)

OUTLINE OF EVENTS: The kingdoms of Syria and Israel attempted to force King Ahaz of Judah to join them in a rebellion against Assyria. Ahaz refused and sent to Assyria for help. Assyria responded and in c.732 sacked both Damascus, the capital of Syria, and Samaria, the capital of Israel. Ten years later the Assyrians returned to finish the destruction of Israel.

It may seem odd, after having sections that have covered hundreds of years of history, suddenly to have a section that covers no more than fifteen years. The reason for this is that the events that led up to Israel, in the north, being destroyed are some of the most important for understanding what happens later and are unknown by many people. It is worth, therefore, going a little more slowly through this history in order to recognize the importance of this particular period.

The countries conquered by Assyria were never very happy about being vassals of this great empire (who would be?) and, from time to time, attempted to rebel. The end of the eighth century seemed a good time for such a rebellion since Assyria was caught up by internal struggles and appeared weaker than it had been. Unfortunately for those rebelling, the end of the eighth century also saw the rise of Tiglath-Pileser III, one of the greatest generals that Assyria had ever had. Their apparent weakness turned out to be a myth.

The events of this period are known by scholars as the Syro-Ephraimite crisis (Syro from Syria and Ephraimite from the alternative name for Israel), since during this period, King Rezin of Syria and King Pekah of Israel attempted to force the young and newly appointed King Ahaz of Judah to join them in rebellion against Assyria. Isaiah 7.1–14 gives us a snapshot of the panic that this move caused in Ahaz. The prophet Isaiah advised Ahaz not to join Syria and Israel in rebellion, but to trust God. Ahaz did neither of these and instead requested help from Assyria.

Assyria clearly recognized the dangers of this rebellion and acted swiftly to suppress it. They swept down from Assyria and sacked both Damascus and Samaria. Israel was allowed to continue in a much reduced state for another ten years but was then besieged and defeated again by Assyria in 722 BC and many of the inhabitants of the land were sent into exile. This event brought about the end of Israel, the Northern Kingdom, as we know it and gave rise to the legend about the lost ten tribes of Israel. These ten tribes disappear from the biblical narrative at this point and various groups such as Beta Israel of Ethiopia or the Igbo Jews of Nigeria trace their heritage back to them. The Samaritans who lived during the time of Jesus (and indeed who still remain today though in a much reduced number) also claim that they were descendants of the destroyed Northern Kingdom of Israel (though this is much disputed by scholars).

From 722 BC onwards the history of the people of God now becomes only the history of Judah, though archaeological evidence suggests that many people from the north fled south to Jerusalem and lived there after the destruction of Israel. The fall of Samaria had an unusual effect on Judah. Rather than terrifying it, it seemed to give rise to greater confidence and the belief that, unlike Israel, God would save Judah from disaster.

Judah on its own

ROUGH HISTORICAL DATE: c.722 to c.597 BC

RECORDED IN 2 Kings 18.11–24, 2 Chronicles 29–36.10, Isaiah 30–1 and 36–9, Jeremiah 1–39

KEY CHARACTERS: Hezekiah, Manasseh, Josiah (kings of Judah), Isaiah, Jeremiah (prophets), Sennacherib (king of Assyria), Pharaoh Necho II (king of Egypt), Nebuchadnezzar (king of Babylon)

OUTLINE OF EVENTS: Following the fall of Samaria, Hezekiah decided to rebel against Assyria. Judah was punished by Assyria but Jerusalem was not destroyed. Towards the end of the seventh century, Assyria's power began to wane and it was eventually defeated by Babylon. Josiah died in battle attempting to thwart a last stand by Assyria and Egypt against Babylon.

As we have just seen, it was Ahaz, king of Judah, who, according to the Bible, set in motion the chain of events that led to the destruction of the Northern Kingdom. When he appealed to Assyria for help against the threat of his northern neighbours (of Israel and Syria), Ahaz appears to have sealed their fate and given Assyria the excuse to destroy the Northern Kingdom. Although Ahaz began this course of events, it was his son Hezekiah who was on the throne in Judah when Israel was finally destroyed in 722 BC. This, however, does not seem to have taught Hezekiah anything.

When Sargon II died, Hezekiah rebelled against Assyria and formed an alliance with Egypt. Sennacherib, Sargon's son, sought revenge by invading Judah in c.701 BC and destroying nearly all the Judean cities. Sennacherib got as far as Jerusalem and besieged the city but, then, suddenly withdrew. 2 Kings attributes this to the intervention of the Angel of the Lord (2 Kings 18–19). The surprising withdrawal is also recorded by the Greek historian Herodotus who attributes it to a plague of mice. Assyrian records suggest it was because Hezekiah started paying his tribute again. Whatever the reason, Jerusalem was saved.

Hezekiah's reign also saw a time of religious reformation. 2 Kings reports approvingly of Hezekiah's attempt to expel foreign religions, to destroy shrines to Israel's God outside of Jerusalem, and to re-institute things like the pilgrimage to Jerusalem at the feast of the Passover.

Hezekiah's reforms were, 2 Kings tells us, overthrown by Hezekiah's son, Manasseh, who had the longest reign – fifty-five years – in the history of Judah. It is clear that Manasseh was hated by the author of 2 Kings, but archaeologists suggest that he was a highly successful king who revived Judah's economy. He was succeeded briefly by his son Amon, who in turned was succeeded by another son of Manasseh, Josiah. Josiah, like Hezekiah, instituted widespread religious reform, including a renovation of the temple during which 'the book of the Law' was found in the temple (2 Kings 22.8). Many scholars believe that at least part of the accounts of Joshua, 1 and 2 Samuel, and 1 and 2 Kings can be traced back to the reign of Josiah and his religious reforms.

Outside of Israel, the Ancient Near East was shifting and changing. The Assyrian Empire was crumbling, and Babylon and Egypt were gaining strength. This meant that for the first time in many years, Judah was able to be relatively independent. This all changed in *c.*609 BC when Egypt decided to go to the aid of ailing Assyria. For some reason, Josiah attempted to prevent the Egyptian army – led by Pharaoh Necho II – from joining the Assyrian army. During this battle, at Megiddo, Josiah was killed and as a result Judah came under the control of Egypt. Following Josiah's death, Judah crowned Jehoahaz as king but he was deposed by Egypt and was replaced by them with his brother Jehoiakim.

In *c.*605 BC the Egyptians were spectacularly defeated by the Babylonians and Jehoiakim switched allegiance to Babylon. Three years later, he switched his allegiance back to Egypt, something which caused the Babylonians to invade Judah and besiege Jerusalem. During the siege Jehoiakim died and was succeeded by his son Jehoiakin (also called Jeconiah). Three months later the city fell and Jehoiakin and many of the king's court, the priests, and other artisans were taken into exile in Babylon, in *c.*597.

This event is known as the Exile, or the Babylonian captivity, and should not be confused with the fall of the Northern Kingdom in 722 BC. Although many Israelites were taken into exile in 722 BC, when people refer to the Exile they mean the Exile to Babylon from Judah.

The Exile

ROUGH HISTORICAL DATE: c.597 to c.538 BC

RECORDED IN 2 Kings 25, 2 Chronicles 36.11–23, Jeremiah 34–52, Lamentations, Ezekiel, Isaiah 40–55

KEY CHARACTERS: Zedekiah (king of Judah), Nebuchadnezzar (king of Babylon), Jeremiah, Ezekiel, Isaiah (prophets), Cyrus II (king of Persia)

OUTLINE OF EVENTS: Jehoiakin's brother, Zedekiah, was made king in his place but later rebelled against the Babylonians causing a second invasion by the Babylonian army and the utter destruction of Jerusalem. At this point the vast majority of Jerusalem's élite were taken away to join the smaller first wave of exiles in Babylon. The Exile came to an end when the Persian Empire under Cyrus II (the Great) conquered the Babylonian Empire.

The Babylonians made Jehoiakin's brother, Zedekiah, king of Judah and left him to govern Judah on their behalf. A few years later, Zedekiah made another alliance with Egypt and rebelled against the Babylonians. Nebuchadnezzar returned and besieged Jerusalem, for about thirty months. Eventually they broke through the walls of Jerusalem, and razed the city to the ground. The temple was destroyed and the vast majority of the élite were taken into exile in Babylon in c.587. The book of Lamentations expresses some of the despair that was felt about the level of this destruction.

The Babylonians appointed Gedaliah, who was not a descendant of David, to govern Judah, so for the first time since the time of David Judah was now ruled by a non-Davidic ruler. Around 582, Yishmael, a descendant of David, supported by a group of Judeans and the king of Ammon, assassinated Gedaliah. Following this, any Jews who remained in Judah feared further reprisals from the Babylonians and fled to Egypt.

This moment marks the end of pre-exilic Judah but it also marks the end of something else as well. Up to this point in the narrative, we have been able to depend primarily on the accounts in the Bible itself to reconstruct the key events in Israel and Judah's history. From now on the task becomes much more complex. The accounts in the major historical books come to an end with the Exile and in what follows we have to resort to piecing together accounts referred to in various books of the Bible as well as books outside of the Bible in order to get a sense of what might have happened when.

The next significant event of the period occurred nearly fifty years later when in 538 the Babylonian Empire was defeated by a new eastern super-power, the Persian Empire, under Cyrus the Great. Cyrus was one of the iconic leaders of his age, and is reputed to have been one of Alexander the Great's heroes. Cyrus reigned for about thirty years. In that space of time he conquered the Median, the Lydian, and then the Babylonian empires, which meant that his empire stretched from the Mediterranean Sea as far as what we would now call the borders of India. Cyrus' descendants, Cambyses I and Darius I, continued his expansion, pushing into Egypt and Greece.

The Persian Empire differed from that of the Babylonians in that the Persians maintained a deep respect for the customs and religions of the countries that they conquered and a belief that both they and the Persians would be best served if they followed their own religion and customs in their own land. As a result, all the Babylonian exiles were encouraged to begin to return to their home territories. This marks the formal end of the exilic period.

The Persian period

ROUGH HISTORICAL DATE: c.538 to c.332 BC

RECORDED IN Haggai, Zechariah, Ezra, Nehemiah

KEY CHARACTERS: Cyrus and Darius (kings of Persia), Zerubbabel, Joshua, Haggai, Zechariah, Ezra, Nehemiah

OUTLINE OF EVENTS: The temple vessels were returned and a decree issued for the rebuilding of the temple but those who attempted to rebuild the temple, and subsequently restore Jerusalem, were met with considerable local opposition.

During the Persian period, the land of Judah became known as Yehud Medinata, a phrase which means simply Province of Judah in Aramaic (a language used across the Persian Empire). Yehud Medinata (often called just Yehud) was a province in the large satrapy of Eber-Nari. The enormous Persian Empire was split into twenty satrapies, and each one was governed by a satrap who, though not a king himself, ruled in place of the king. The satrapy of Eber-Nari, which meant literally beyond the river, refers to a region that covers modern Israel, Jordan, Lebanon and Syria.

The events surrounding the return of the Jews to Yehud are hazy and difficult to reconstruct from the scant sources available. The book of Ezra refers to someone called Sheshbazzar, a prince of Judah, to whom Cyrus is said to have entrusted the temple vessels so that he could return to Yehud. What is unclear is what happened to him and the vessels. The next characters mentioned are Zerubbabel (a grandson of Jehoiakin) and Joshua (a priest).

Some think that Sheshbazzar and Zerubbabel were the same person; others that Sheshbazzar was some kind of relative of Zerubbabel (possibly uncle) whom Zerubbabel replaced when he returned to the land; and others still that Sheshbazzar somehow mysteriously vanished and was only later replaced by Zerubbabel.

The books of Haggai, Zechariah, Ezra and Nehemiah all refer to the return of a large number of exiles with Zerubbabel and Joshua. This is likely to be dated to around 520 BC. According to the books of Ezra and Nehemiah, the attempts to rebuild the land were constantly opposed by the 'people of the land' (e.g. Ezra 4.4) and the governor of Eber-Nari (Ezra 4.11–12). Who these people were is not clear, but the most likely explanation is that they were the people of Judah who were left behind and not taken into Exile. In fact, it was only due to the intervention of Darius I that the temple was finally completed in 515 BC. The completion of the temple was a significant moment in this part of the history of Yehud, not least because it marks the start of a new phase in history. When scholars talk about the period that runs from Haggai to the Jewish War in 67–72 AD they usually call it the 'Second Temple Period' in homage to the completion of the temple which marked Judah's second temple after the first one built by King Solomon.

One of the great mysteries of the post-exilic period was what happened to the Davidic line. We know that they returned to Yehud (since both Sheshbazzar and Zerubbabel are referred to), but what happened next is hard to discern. Some think that a restored Davidic line ruled until around 500 BC but then petered out, others that it never succeeded in getting re-established in the first place. If this is the case then it may be that the Davidic kings were blamed for the exile and so were never trusted again after the return from Babylon. Whatever the truth of the matter, the Davidic line was never properly re-established in Yehud.

There is, after Haggai and Zechariah, a gap in the history until nearly a hundred years later when Ezra and Nehemiah were commissioned to rebuild the temple and restore the whole of the city of Jerusalem. It is not easy to tell whether Ezra and Nehemiah were in Yehud at the same time as each other or whether the account has been conflated to give the impression of a seamless whole. This is one of a number of issues from this period about which scholars cannot agree; either way their dates were probably sometime between 458 and 444 BC.

The official narrative of the Bible falls silent at this point and any reconstruction of events must rely on fragmentary evidence from the prophets, the books of Daniel and Esther (which were probably written a long time after the period they describe), and various external texts (like, for example, the histories of the Jewish historian Flavius Josephus who wrote towards the end of the first century AD). Even though the subsequent period of history is not covered in the Bible, it is vital for understanding the development of Judaism and Christianity in this period.

The Greek period

ROUGH HISTORICAL DATE: c. 332 to c. 164 BC

RECORDED IN no biblical text, though thought to lie behind the book of Daniel

KEY CHARACTERS: Alexander the Great, Antiochus IV (Epiphanes), Mattathias ben Johanan, Judas Maccabee

OUTLINE OF EVENTS: Alexander conquered a vast empire but on his death his empire split into four. Judea was ruled first by the Egyptian Ptolemaic Empire and then by the Syrian Seleucid Empire until the Maccabean Revolt in 164 BC.

The next great phase of history sees the invasion by yet another empire and this time the name of the country translated into

Greek: Judea. For the first time an invading empire came from the west and not from the east. Alexander the Great swept through the Persian Empire, conquering it and bringing with him Greek culture and language. Alexander was one of the greatest military rulers of the Ancient world and by the age of thirty had established an empire that stretched from the Ionian Sea to the Himalayas. He died, undefeated, in 323 BC at the age of thirty-two.

As with many great, and rapidly won, empires, the Greek Empire could not withstand the loss of its great leader and as a result, after forty years of conflict, split into four major power blocks: the Seleucid Empire (based in Syria but stretching across the East), the Ptolemaic Empire (based in Egypt), the Pergamum kingdom based in Asia Minor, and Macedon in Greece. This is known as the period of the Diadochi (a Greek word meaning successors).

At the start of the Hellenistic period Judah fell under the control of the Ptolemaic kingdom from Egypt. Although the Ptolemies are not well known, they did have one very famous ruler, Cleopatra VII (69–30 BC), who sided with Mark Anthony against Julius Caesar and was the last Ptolemaic ruler before their defeat by the Romans. Long before Cleopatra, however, the Ptolemies lost control of the kingdom of Judah to the neighbouring Seleucid Empire in around 200 BC. The succession of Antiochus IV Epiphanes to the Seleucid throne radically changed Judah's future.

Antiochus did not comprehend (or chose not to) that Judea could not be ruled like any other part of the Seleucid Hellenistic kingdom. He undertook a policy that began with the attempt to usurp the High Priest and ended with a decree which forbade Jews from any form of Jewish religious practice and the insistence that they sacrificed to Greek gods instead. This sparked a rebellion led by Mattathias ben Johanan which was later picked up by his son Judas.

The Hasmonean period

ROUGH HISTORICAL DATE: c.164 to c.63 BC

RECORDED IN no canonical biblical text, though they form the background and context of 1 and 2 Maccabees (a Greek translation of the Old Testament); also recorded in the writings of the Jewish historian Josephus

KEY CHARACTERS: Judas Maccabee, Jonathan Maccabee

OUTLINE OF EVENTS: The Maccabee brothers defeated the Seleucid army and ruled Judea semi-independently as the Hasmonean dynasty for about the next hundred years.

Judas led an army which gained the name of the Maccabees (which some think comes from the Hebrew word for hammer). In 164 BC Judas' army succeeded in defeating the Seleucid army (part of the reason for this being the growing threat of Rome to the Hellenistic kingdoms which weakened them considerably) and Judas' brother Jonathan was made high priest in the temple. This is the origin of the great Jewish feast of Hanukkah. The Maccabees continued to be leaders and high priests for the next hundred years and became known as the Hasmoneans, and the period as the Hasmonean period.

One of the key events of the Hasmonean period was the re-annexation of a number of regions around Judea, including the Galilee region (where Jesus of Nazareth came from) and Idumea (where Herod the Great came from). It is not entirely clear when this happened though a good guess is around 100 BC. After this conversion many Jews emigrated particularly to the Galilee so that by the time of the New Testament the Galilee was predominantly Jewish.

The Roman period

ROUGH HISTORICAL DATE: c.63 BC to c.70 AD

RECORDED IN the writings of the Jewish historian Josephus as well as in the New Testament (though there with a particular focus on the life of Jesus)

KEY CHARACTERS: Herod the Great, Herod Antipas, Philip the Tetrarch, Herod Archelaus, Pilate, Jesus of Nazareth, Herod Agrippa I

OUTLINE OF EVENTS: The Romans invaded in 63 BC and ruled the region either directly or through Herod the Great (or one of his successors) until the Jewish War in 66–73 AD.

The Romans first entered Judea as a result of a conflict between two brothers of the Hasmonean dynasty: Hyrcanus II and Aristobulus II. They were invited into the region to help Aristobulus (but then made Hyrcanus ruler, though not king). Hyrcanus was succeeded by one of his courtiers, Antipater the Idumean, whose son Herod the Great was declared king of the Jews by the Romans. Herod's tenuous claim to power made him a paranoid and brutal ruler who was prepared to kill even his own beloved wife when she became too popular.

Roman Judea was split between three of Herod's sons after his death. Herod Archelaus was given half of the kingdom, and the other half was split between Philip the Tetrarch and Herod Antipas.

Herod Archelaus was such a bad ruler that he was deposed by the Romans at the request of his own people (the people of Judea), and from then on the region was governed directly by a Roman Prefect (the most well-known being Pontius Pilate). Both Philip and Herod Antipas continued to rule until 34 and 39 AD respectively when their territories too were governed directly by Rome. Between 41 and 44 BC much of the land was governed by

Herod the Great's grandson, Herod Agrippa. Otherwise the region was governed directly by the Romans until the first Jewish–Roman war of 66–73 AD.

THE FIRST JEWISH–ROMAN WAR

The first Jewish–Roman war, although not directly mentioned in the New Testament, is one of the most important events of the period. According to the Jewish historian Josephus, it began in 66 AD in Caesarea (a Roman coastal colony just south of the Galilee) as the result of a skirmish between Greeks and Jews. This quickly escalated into attacks on Romans themselves and overt challenges towards their authority. Eventually the Romans arrested and crucified a number of Jewish leaders in Jerusalem and at that point various nationalist, anti-Roman factions joined together and took up arms.

Early on in the war, the Jewish rebels soundly defeated the Roman army at Beth-Horon. This was regarded by the Romans as one of the worst defeats by rebels in the whole of their Roman history but also opened up a new phase in the war. Following this defeat the Romans appointed a general, Vespasian, and in 67 AD he landed in Egypt. Together with his son Titus, Vespasian defeated the Galilee.

One of the defeated Galilean leaders was Josephus who promptly changed sides and was taken as a prisoner to Rome. Indeed one of the problems we have in working out exactly what happened in the War is that the major source for the period was written by Josephus who was clearly biased.

After the defeat of the Galilee Vespasian returned to Rome where he was popularly acclaimed as emperor and his son, Titus, continued fighting. Although most of Judea was quite easily con-quered, the zealots held out in Rome until 70 AD when, eventually, the city was breached by the Romans and the temple destroyed. Some Jewish rebels held out for a few more years. The most famous of these are those who fled to Masada – a high mountain in the Judean desert – and opposed the Romans for a further two years, until the Romans broke through only to discover that the roughly 960 inhabitants had all committed suicide.

The first Jewish–Roman war ended in a defeat for the Jewish people and the scattering of many Jews across the Roman Empire as they were sold into slavery by the Romans. Two more, smaller Jewish–Roman wars in 115–17 and 132–5 resulted in the Emperor Hadrian's attempt to root out Judaism with enormous cruelty. This also resulted in the Jewish people being scattered across the Roman Empire and only very few Jewish communities remaining in the land.

The story of the people of God as recorded in the Bible covers nearly 2000 years of history and many miles of geography from Babylon to Egypt. Although it is the history of a relatively small number of people (comparatively speaking) it is a history which touches and is touched by great empires which, in their day, dominated world history. The story that begins with the calling of Abraham and ends with the scattering of the Jews from Judea is a story of continuing political and historic importance which was far from over, even when the biblical narrative lapsed into silence.

2

Genre

Imagine sitting down and picking up a telephone directory and beginning to read from the beginning to the end. Or again imagine picking up a novel and dipping into it, reading a paragraph from page 56, then one from page 23, and another from page 98. No one in their right mind would even consider doing this, yet this, or the equivalent, is often what people do when they begin to read the Bible. The challenge is to be able to work out what we are reading, and therefore how we should approach it. We know this and usually when we read something we work out automatically – even if we do it subconsciously – what kind of a book we have in our hands and what we are reading it for. We then adapt the way in which we read to the kind of book we are reading.

This is as important to do while reading the Bible as it is when we read any other book. The problem we face, however, is that the Bible isn't really one book but lots of different kinds of books all woven together. As a result, if we read it as though it were a single book which we should read in a single way, we immediately run into difficulties. Only the most dedicated of readers can make it through books like Leviticus, which are collections of laws all gathered together, when they are reading the Bible as though it is a novel beginning with Genesis and ending with Revelation. In the same kind of way, some people struggle to understand books like Mark's Gospel because they dip into it a few verses at a time and read them out of order.

The problem is that the name 'the Bible' suggests that it is a single book and should be read like one; whereas in reality it is a collection of different books of different kinds. The problem actually lies in our English title. We get our English name for the

Bible from one of the earliest Greek titles used by Christians to refer to their Scriptures. The Greek title was '*ta Biblia*'. This word is plural and means simply 'the books'. This title accurately prepares us for the fact that what we are going to read will contain a variety of styles and, as a result, might require us to read its contents in different ways. In contrast our English 'the Bible' suggests a more coherent, single style.

One of the key things to bear in mind, then, when preparing to read the Bible is that in the course of its sixty-six books you will come across a wide variety of different types of books: from law codes to history; from poetry to prose; from books that provide information to those that stir the soul; from letters to sermons. The Bible contains different kinds of writings and we need to be prepared to read them in different ways. Some books are better read from beginning to end in one sitting; whereas other books are best understood if dipped into for information; some other books, again, are best read in chunks. The key thing is to recognize what type of a book each book is and then to read it accordingly. Some of the books, or even parts of books, are easy to read and can be understood straight away; others, however, feel more alien to the modern mind and take some time for us to work out what they are trying to say.

The Bible as a library

The Bible is often described as being more like a library than a book. Like a library, it contains a wide range of different kinds of books, and sometimes even different kinds of writings within a single book. As with all libraries it helps the user if the different kinds of books can be gathered into some kind of order so that the reader can find what they are looking for more easily. Also as librarians will tell you, categorizing books is no easy task. Some books fall into more than one category, and some apparently

don't fall easily into any category. The person cataloguing or categorizing the books often has to decide where to put a book and
others may or may not agree with them. This is as true in the
Bible as it is in any other kind of library.

There are all sorts of different ways of categorizing the biblical books but the main ones include:

- Law – the Bible contains a wide variety of material which
  offers instruction about the way to worship God and to live
  life and can be found primarily in Exodus, Leviticus, Numbers
  and Deuteronomy.
- Historical books – one of the main themes of the Old Testament
  is the telling of the story of the people of God, looking at
  where they came from and how they came to be where they
  are now. The historical books are primarily Judges, Joshua,
  1 and 2 Samuel, 1 and 2 Kings and 1 and 2 Chronicles.
- Worship – another main type of material is worship. The biggest collection of this in the Bible can be found in the Psalms
  which consists of poems or songs used in worship but examples of this kind of material can be found elsewhere throughout the Bible, for example in Exodus 15 or Jonah 2.
- Prophetic writings – the Prophetic writings contain communication from God to his people. There are three major
  prophetic books (Isaiah, Ezekiel and Jeremiah) and 12 minor
  ones (Hosea, Joel, Amos, Obadiah, Jonah, Micah, Nahum,
  Habakkuk, Zephaniah, Haggai, Zechariah and Malachi).
- Wisdom teaching – wisdom teaching is concerned with education in its widest form. Wisdom literature offers teaching
  on how to live life well and can be found primarily in
  Proverbs, Ecclesiastes and Job. The Psalms and the Song of
  Songs are also associated with wisdom.
- Visionary material – this type of writing, often called Jewish
  Apocalyptic, became very popular in the Second Temple
  period and is one of the few types of literature that spans

both the Old and the New Testaments. These kind of writings contain visions of heaven, of angels, and of God sitting on his throne and can be found in Zechariah 9–14, in Daniel 7–12 and, of course, the book of Revelation in the New Testament.

- Gospels – the Gospels (Matthew, Mark, Luke and John), which contain stories of Jesus' life, could be placed with historical books but are so unusual that they are best in their own category.
- Letters – all the letters in the Bible can be found in the New Testament. The most well-known are by Paul the apostle but there are others as well, attributed to people like Peter, James and John, and all written to Christian communities in the first century after Jesus' death.
- Sermon – one book that was traditionally viewed as a letter is now thought by many to be, instead, a sermon. Hebrews in the New Testament may be an early sermon to a group of Jewish Christians.

As we noted above, not all the Bible's writings fall easily into these groups. Books like the much-loved book of Ruth and the book of Esther, which are both stories about influential women in the history of God's people, do not really fall into any of the categories above. The stories are too personal (and some argue too hard to date historically) to place them in the history category but they do not quite fit elsewhere. Their presence suggests that we might need another category entitled 'Stories' or something similar. The problem is that the category 'Stories' could have over half of the Bible in it. Legendary narratives might be another option though this title suggests that there are questions about their historicity which might make some people feel uncomfortable. It is also worth noting those books which are hard to shoe-horn into only one list, such as a number of wisdom Psalms and the Song of Songs both of which appear to straddle two categories: wisdom and poetry.

Ancient cataloguing systems for the books of the Bible

The attempt to categorize the books of the Bible is not new. In fact, the books of the Bible have always been placed in rough categories and these categories affect the way in which the books are read. One of the earliest, and most important, examples of this is the Old Testament itself, which in Hebrew has three main sections. In fact, Jews often called the Hebrew Bible the *Tanakh*, after these three sections. The three sections are:

- The Law (Torah)
- The Prophets (Nevi'im)
- The Writings (Ketuvim)

If you put the first letter of each of Torah, Nevi'im and Ketuvim together you get Tanakh. The Jewish name for the Bible makes very clear that these categories are important for reading and understanding it.

Christians, however, have a different ordering for their books. The Christian Old Testament does not have the same order, or categories, for its books and as a result Christians have read them differently. The Christian Old Testament uses the same order as the Vulgate (the Latin translation of the Bible produced primarily by St Jerome in the fourth century AD) which in turn uses the order of the Septuagint (the Greek translation of the Old Testament which was produced around the second century BC). In fact, there is a custom these days to use the name 'Hebrew Bible' or 'Hebrew Scriptures' to refer to what Christians call the Old Testament in honour of the fact that the books do not just belong to Christians. The problem with this, however, is that not only do Christians not read the text in Hebrew but they do not read the books in the same order as they are in the Tanakh, nor with the same interpretative lens either. As a result, it is a moot point whether they are in fact reading the Hebrew Scriptures or the

Christian Old Testament. As a result of this, throughout most of this book, I shall refer to the books as the Old Testament by way of acknowledging that most of the readers of this book will be reading the books in English in the order found in the Christian Bible not in the Hebrew Tanakh. I will however use the term Hebrew Scriptures whenever I am referring specifically to the Hebrew version of what Christians call the Old Testament.

The Hebrew categories of law, prophets and writings are quite vague but nevertheless significant for understanding the text.

The Law (Torah)

The first thing to notice is that the first five books of the Bible are all gathered together under the heading 'law'. Some of these are very clearly law (for example the books of Leviticus and Deuteronomy are full of laws) but others of them contain stories, some poetry, and family trees (often called genealogies). The importance of this is that if you read Genesis as though it is law it becomes a very different book than if you read it as though it is stories or even history. Reading the book of Genesis as law means that the stories it tells communicate something about how you should live your life, just like Leviticus does. Leviticus shapes the way a person lives their life with a string of commands; Genesis shapes the way a person lives their life by holding up pictures of the way others have lived their lives and leaving the reader to draw appropriate conclusions about what this might mean for them.

Christians no longer call these five books the 'Torah' or law; the most common Christian name for the first five books is 'Pentateuch' which means five teachings. Christian tradition, therefore, avoids saying what the content of these five books are beyond the fact that they contain teaching.

The Prophets

Probably the biggest difference between the way that Jews and Christians read the books of the Hebrew Scriptures/Old Testament is the attitude towards some of the books that in the Hebrew Scriptures are collected together as 'Prophets'. Of course both treat the three Major Prophets (Isaiah, Jeremiah and Ezekiel) and the twelve Minor Prophets (Hosea, Joel, Amos, Obadiah, Jonah, Micah, Nahum, Habakkuk, Zephaniah, Haggai, Zechariah and Malachi) as prophets. The difference occurs in the treatment of Joshua, Judges, 1 and 2 Samuel, and 1 and 2 Kings. Christian tradition treats these as historical books (in other words books which tell the reader what has happened), whereas Jewish tradition treats them as prophecy (in other words as what will happen if the people continue to behave as they have been doing). Treating these books as prophecy means that Joshua, Judges, 1 and 2 Samuel, and 1 and 2 Kings are all read with the end of 2 Kings (i.e. the Judean Exile to Babylon) in mind. This means that there is an grim inevitability to the exile, since it is clear from the opening pages of Joshua onwards both that the covenant between God and God's people will be fractured if they do not obey the commandments and that the people of God do not and cannot obey the commandments. Reading the so-called historical books as prophecy means that we read the stories that they contain in an entirely different way.

The Writings

The least coherent of the collections in the Hebrew Scriptures is the Writings. There are three poetic books (Psalms, Proverbs and Job); five scrolls, known in Hebrew as the *Hamesh Megillot* (Song of Songs, Ruth, Lamentations, Ecclesiastes and Esther) and three other writings (Daniel, Ezra/Nehemiah and 1 and 2 Chronicles). Even the smaller collections only hang together loosely and, unlike with the other collections, there was never any agreement about the final order for this collection. Just as the way the Tanakh orders the books of the Bible tells us much about how these books were read and interpreted within Jewish communities, the Christian Old Testament gathers the books in a certain order that tells us something about how they were read and understood. In the Christian Old Testament the order is as follows:

Genesis	Very early history
Exodus	
Leviticus	Law
Numbers	
Deuteronomy	
Joshua	History
Judges	
Ruth	
1 and 2 Samuel	
1 and 2 Kings	
1 and 2 Chronicles	
Ezra	
Nehemiah	
Esther	
Job	Poetry/Wisdom
Psalms	
Proverbs	
Ecclesiastes	
Song of Solomon	
Isaiah	Prophets
Jeremiah	

Lamentations
Ezekiel
Daniel
Hosea
Joel
Amos
Obadiah
Jonah
Micah
Nahum
Habakkuk
Zephaniah
Haggai
Zechariah
Malachi

If there is a structure to the ordering of the Old Testament it is a roughly chronological one, although this breaks down in the Minor Prophets, tracing history from the origins of the world to the exile and back again.

It is worth noting that this order gives a different significance to certain books. So for example the book of Daniel is treated like a prophet rather than one of the writings; so too the book of Lamentations is more closely allied with Jeremiah (who was traditionally believed to have written Lamentations) than in the Hebrew collections. Also intriguing is the fact that the books of Esther and Ruth are treated more as history than they are in the Hebrew collections.

In the New Testament the order of the books is less significant, though they are still grouped together so that they are in similar type collections, like this:

| Matthew | Lives of Jesus and the Early Church |
| Mark | |

Luke
John
Acts of the Apostles

Romans   Letters of Paul
1 and 2 Corinthians
Galatians
Ephesians
Philippians
Colossians
1 and 2 Thessalonians
1 and 2 Timothy
Titus
Philemon
Hebrews

James   Other Epistles
1 and 2 Peter
1, 2 and 3 John
Jude

Revelation   An Apocalypse

All of this illustrates the importance of trying to work out
what kind of book the book we are reading is, and even what *kinds*
of a book it might be, since that may well affect how we read it.

The shelves of the Bible's library

One of the best ways to get a sense of what any library has in
stock is to browse along its shelves, to see what sections it has and
to look at the kinds of books it has in those sections. The same is
true of the Bible. One of the best ways of getting a sense of what
it is like is to browse its sections for a while and by doing so to
get a sense of the kind of books it contains.

Law

FOUND IN: Exodus, Leviticus, Numbers and Deuteronomy

OUTLINE: Basic laws governing worship in the temple and the behaviour of God's people as a sign of their covenant relationship

POSSIBLE DATES OF COMPOSITION: *c.*600–500 BC

Admittedly law is not the most exciting place to begin our browsing of the biblical books but it does take us right to the heart of some of the key issues of the Bible. The laws of the Old Testament are integrally related to the Old Testament theology of covenant. The covenant established a relationship between God and God's people which involved obligations on both sides. Put simply the covenant was stated as 'I will be your God and you will be my people'. Implicit in this is an expectation of continued relationship and exclusivity. God would choose no other people and the people would choose no other Gods. An expression of the people's continued commitment to the covenant was their keeping of the laws that we find in the pages of the Old Testament. It is a common, normally Christian, misconception that Jewish understanding of law is driven by legalism. In reality it is not; Jewish understanding of the law is much less about keeping law for law's sake than it is about human welfare. Indeed a famous medieval rabbi called Maimonides argued that the Torah was concerned with the welfare of both the body and the soul (*Guide for the Perplexed* 3:27).

One important point to notice, though, is that although the laws are extensive they are not complete. It would be almost impossible to craft your life solely on the laws that we find in the Old Testament. In fact, it is clear that there were laws that governed everyday life that are simply not in the law books. A good example of this is property law. In Jeremiah 32.11, the prophet refers to buying a field and to taking the deeds of the property, whereas there is no reference in the law codes to the drawing up of such deeds. Indeed there are so many gaps in the laws that a tradition of oral law grew up in Judaism. This is called in Hebrew Halakhah and stands alongside the written law or Torah. Jewish tradition states that God gave Moses two collections of laws on Mount Sinai; one was written down (Torah) and the other was passed on by word of mouth (Halakhah). It is said that the Halakhah was written down in 200 AD as the Mishnah in the form of the sayings of the Rabbis. The content of the Mishnah in many ways plugged the gaps in the written law and helped people to keep the laws more fully.

The law books, to put it mildly, are not easy to read. This, however, is part of the point. They were not designed to be narratives read as though they were a novel (although intriguingly the laws in Exodus and Deuteronomy are embedded in a narrative). Instead they are designed to be reference books which laid out the parameters of existence, and to which God's people would return again and again to clarify the implications of what they contained.

There are numerous different collections of law in the Old Testament. The best known of these are the 'Ten Commandments' found in Exodus 20.1–17 and repeated in Deuteronomy 5.6–21. Alongside these are the Covenant Code in Exodus 20.22–23.19, the miscellaneous collection of laws in the book of Numbers, and the two major collections of law found in Deuteronomy and Leviticus. Many scholars regard the laws of Deuteronomy and Leviticus as coming from different traditions. Although the laws in Leviticus and Deuteronomy are similar in that each book contains an extensive and detailed description of law, there the similarity ends.

The laws in Deuteronomy are thought to come from a 'Deuteronomic tradition' which may also lie behind Joshua, 1 and 2 Samuel, and 1 and 2 Kings. The emphasis in this tradition is on the covenant between God and the people and the importance of keeping the law as a part of this. In contrast the laws in Leviticus are thought to come from a 'priestly tradition' and are much more concerned with worship in the temple in Jerusalem and, in particular, with the sacrifices that took place in the temple.

It is hard to date these collections. Few scholars think any of these, including the Ten Commandments, originate from the time of Moses. The earliest collection of laws may well be the Covenant Code which contains laws that govern what people do while living in settled communities. For example Exodus 22.5 contains laws about letting a vineyard grow over, which would have had little significance for people wandering in the wilderness (as they were during the time of Moses when this code purports to be set). This has led some scholars to suggest that the collection dates to around the twelfth–eleventh centuries BC, though others would trace its roots even earlier than this. The major collections of Deuteronomy and Leviticus are thought to come from a much later period. Deuteronomy may be dated to around the seventh–sixth centuries and Leviticus to around the sixth–fifth centuries.

Historical books

FOUND IN: Joshua, Judges, 1 and 2 Samuel, 1 and 2 Kings (and possibly also Jeremiah), 1 and 2 Chronicles, Ezra, Nehemiah

OUTLINE: Telling the story of God's people from the settlement in the land under Joshua to the rebuilding of the city walls after the Exile under Nehemiah

POSSIBLE DATE OF COMPOSITION: Deuteronomistic histories c.700–600 BC
The Chronicler and Ezra-Nehemiah c.400–300 BC

The historical books fall into two major collections: the Deuteronomistic histories and the Writings of the Chronicler.

The Deuteronomistic histories

The Deuteronomistic histories simply refers to a collection of books – Joshua, Judges, 1 and 2 Samuel, and 1 and 2 Kings – which all seem to be written in a similar style. The reason why they have been given such a tongue-twisting name by Old Testament scholars is because the style of writing they contain and the theology they put forward is very similar to that in the book of Deuteronomy. One of the main focuses of Deuteronomy is the law that needs to be followed, but more important even than that, the catastrophic consequences involved in not keeping it sufficiently.

The books of Joshua, Judges, 1 and 2 Samuel, and 1 and 2 Kings trace the story of God's people from the time when they first entered the Promised Land under Joshua to the time when vast numbers of them were forced to leave again under the Babylonians. As a result, it becomes clear that one of the major questions in these books is what went wrong. What happened to the people that God had promised to love and save so that eventually they had to leave the land that they believed God had given to them? In fact it seems likely that these books were written from the time of the Exile in Babylon looking backwards from that catastrophe in the sixth century BC and telling a story of how it is that God's people got there.

It should be noted, however, that this does not mean that all these books were written by the same hand. Indeed, these historical books show evidence of preserving more than one opinion on certain matters. Most striking of all is the fact that 1 Samuel preserves two different views on whether having a king is a good idea. So 1 Samuel 8 has the prophet Samuel opposed to the Israelites having a king and presents the case against having a king, and 1 Samuel 9–10 describes Samuel spontaneously anointing Saul as king on God's instruction.

The Chronicler and Ezra-Nehemiah

One of the confusing features of the Bible is that, more than once, there are apparent repetitions of material. One of the most obvious places for this is in the books of 1 and 2 Chronicles. Here we find for the most part a repetition of material in 1 and 2 Samuel and 1 and 2 Kings. Indeed, it seems likely that the writer of 1 and 2 Chronicles used the Deuteronomistic histories as a source.

They aren't, however, exactly the same. 1 and 2 Chronicles seem connected in some way with the books of Ezra–Nehemiah (in fact Ezra–Nehemiah are best regarded as a single book as they are so closely connected), and hence together tell the story from David to the rebuilding of the walls of Jerusalem after the exile. The major difference between 1 and 2 Chronicles and 1 and 2 Samuel/1 and 2 Kings is that the focus of the Chronicler is almost entirely the Southern Kingdom of Judah rather than on the Northern and Southern Kingdoms as in the other writings. Another key difference is that whereas 2 Kings ends as the people go into exile, 2 Chronicles ends with Cyrus, king of Persia's decree that the exiles should return home. The perspective of the two stories, then, is different. 2 Kings ends in the despair of exile; 2 Chronicles in the hope of a new future.

The decree at the end of 2 Chronicles is repeated at the start of the book of Ezra, a feature that suggests that 1 and 2 Chronicles and Ezra–Nehemiah are to be regarded as connected in some way. Despite this, however, there are enough differences between the two to suggest that although they have some connection they probably came from different authors. The reference to Cyrus' decrees indicates that both 1 and 2 Chronicles and Ezra–Nehemiah were written after 538 BC and many scholars today would date them to between the fourth and third centuries BC.

Worship

FOUND IN: the Psalms, and a few additional chapters throughout the Bible

OUTLINE: poems/songs addressed to God as part of public or private worship

POSSIBLE DATES OF COMPOSITION: a wide range of dates from c.1000–200 BC

The Psalms vie with the book of Isaiah for being the best known of Old Testament texts among Christians. The book of Psalms is the largest collection of poetic texts of worship in the Old Testament, though there are many other similar poetic texts that can be found in the middle of other narratives, like Miriam's song of praise after the crossing of the Red Sea (Exodus 15) or Jonah's lament in the belly of the big fish (Jonah 2). The Psalms were probably most often used in the worship of the temple in Jerusalem, and often refer to musical accompaniment on trumpets, lutes, harps, tambourines, strings, pipes and cymbals (see Psalm 150). The evidence throughout the Old Testament, however, suggests that they were also used in private devotion. For example the book of Jonah has Jonah reciting a Psalm of lament in the belly of the big fish, when one can presume that there were not many other people around!

The Psalter, or book of Psalms, is made up of five collections of Psalms. Each collection ends with a doxology, i.e. an expression of praise to God (e.g. Psalm 41.13: 'Blessed be the LORD, the God of Israel, from everlasting to everlasting. Amen and Amen'; others can be found at 72.18–19, 89.52, 106.48). The last Psalm of all, Psalm 150, is one long doxology which completes the collection as a whole.

The obvious question to ask is when this collection first happened and, somewhat inevitably, there is not much evidence that points to a date. It is nevertheless interesting to notice that 1 Chronicles 16.8–36 quotes from parts of Psalms 105 and 106 ending with a doxology. This suggests that the collection is already in place when 1 Chronicles is written (otherwise they might not have included the doxology) so it would suggest that the Psalms have been gathered together by the early post-exilic period (so sometime before the fourth century BC). They probably came together over a long period of time and it is likely that these five collections of Psalms (1–41; 42–72; 73–89; 90–106, 107–150) were made up from collections that already existed. One of the things that points to this is that some Psalms are repeated (e.g. Psalm 53 is a repetition of Psalm 14) which suggests that they existed in more than one previously existing collection. So, when the all five collections were gathered together the Psalms that were repeated in different collections were kept in each of those collections and ended up being repeated. Over half of the Psalms have headings ascribing them to King David (others are attributed to much less well-known figures such as Jeduthun or Ethan the Ezrahite) but few scholars today think that David actually wrote them. Instead they regard them as arising out of the tradition of David's devotion and musicality and written as a tribute to him.

Prophetic writings

FOUND IN: Isaiah, Jeremiah, Ezekiel, Hosea, Joel, Amos, Obadiah, Jonah, Micah, Nahum, Habakkuk, Zephaniah, Haggai, Zechariah, Malachi

OUTLINE: messages of warning and/or encouragement to God's people

POSSIBLE DATES OF COMPOSITION: a wide range of dates from c.800–500 BC

The book of Isaiah, alongside the Psalms, is one of the most read books in the Christian Old Testament, so much so that some even call it the fifth gospel. What they mean by this is that Isaiah has so many prophecies in it that are interpreted by Christians as relating to Christ that it might as well be bound alongside the gospels in the New Testament. Although the most important for Christians, Isaiah is not the only prophetic book. There are many others as well. The prophetic writings purport to be the words of God spoken through an individual to God's people and the majority of prophecy is written in the style of poetry, rather than prose. It is worth remembering, however, that the prophetic books are not the only place where prophets are mentioned in the Old Testament. In the historical books, particularly 1 and 2 Samuel and 1 and 2 Kings, there are numerous stories about what various prophets (like Nathan, Elijah or Elisha) did but little about what they said; in contrast the prophetic books contain what prophets like Ezekiel, Amos and Odadiah said but very little about what they did.

Although prophecy is traditionally associated with telling the future, most prophets are more concerned with speaking out – forth telling rather than foretelling. In other words, much of what prophets say are messages to their contemporaries about what they are currently doing and what consequences might lie in store if they do not change. The two major most often repeated condemnations of the people by the prophets is that they are not worshipping God as they should and, equally importantly, that they are not caring for their neighbours. Prophets like Hosea and Amos are particularly associated with critiquing the people for abusing the poor who lived in their midst. The prophets' messages, however, were not all gloom. Although they prophesied a catastrophic future if the people did not change their ways, beyond that catastrophe many of the prophets pointed to a time of peace, prosperity and hope.

The earliest of the prophets, whose prophetic writings have been preserved, prophesied in the eighth century BC: Hosea and

Amos to the people of the north and Micah and Isaiah to the people of the south. Jeremiah and Ezekiel prophesied in the late seventh and early sixth centuries to a people about to go into Exile (and then who did go into Exile). Others, like Haggai and Zechariah, prophesied to those just returning from exile in the late sixth centuries. Others still are very hard to date since they prophesied more general messages.

Within Judaism it is believed that prophecy ended with Ezra, which is why there are no more prophetic texts after the fourth century BC (and also why Daniel, which many believe to be written in the second century BC, is not thought to be a prophet). In Christianity there are varying views. Some agree that prophecy ended, while others argue that it continued and is still possible today.

Wisdom teaching

FOUND IN: Job, Proverbs, Ecclesiastes, Song of Songs/ Solomon as well as some Psalms, and Wisdom of Solomon, Sirach in the Apocrypha

OUTLINE: reflections on living wisely

POSSIBLE DATES OF COMPOSITION: a wide range of dates from c.500–200 BC (though may contain earlier traditions)

The books that are often labelled as 'wisdom material' are called this because, unsurprisingly enough, they express an interest in the concept of wisdom and how to find it. Within the Old Testament the books of Proverbs, Job and Ecclesiastes (which is sometimes also called by its Hebrew name Qoheleth, rather than its Greek name Ecclesiastes) are regarded by everyone as being wisdom literature and the Song of Songs and Lamentations are also thought by some to be part of this tradition. There are also a number of Psalms like 1, 19, 37, 73 and 119 which are thought to be Wisdom Psalms, and some texts from the Apocrypha which fit into the category of Wisdom. The Wisdom of Solomon, Sirach (sometimes also called Ecclesiasticus) and possibly the book of Tobit are also considered part of this material (for more on what the Apocrypha is, see chapter 3).

Some of these writings are concerned with education. For example the book of Proverbs contains the command 'Hear, my child, your father's instruction, and do not reject your mother's teaching' (Proverbs 1.8) which implies that it contains material that will be used to educate children in the right way to think and act. Indeed much of the book of Proverbs is concerned with an exploration of the best way to live in the world. What is less clear is where this education took place. Some think that it was used generally within the family, whereas others argue that it would have been used in the king's court to educate young noble men or in schools of some variety.

One of the striking features of Proverbs, in particular, is that wisdom is not described as an abstract idea but as a person. Abstract nouns, like wisdom which in Hebrew is *hokhmah* and in Greek *sophia*, are always feminine (as indeed are the nouns for love, peace, joy etc.); as a result wisdom, particularly in Proverbs and the Wisdom of Solomon, is depicted as a woman.

A major theme in wisdom literature is blessedness (which is sometimes translated as happiness); so for example Psalm 1 begins 'Happy are those who do not follow the advice of the wicked, or take the path that sinners tread, or sit in the seat of scoffers; but their delight is in the law of the LORD, and on his law they meditate day and night' (Psalm 1.1–2). In other words, the wisdom writers seem to believe that happiness was bound up with living in the right kind of way. The significant exception to this is the book of Job which acts as a fundamental challenge to this way of thinking. The book depicts Job as a righteous man who suffered despite living a good and upright life. This indicates that wisdom literature could critique itself from within.

Another anomaly of the wisdom material is the Song of Songs. Although often included in lists of wisdom material, it is nothing like the other texts; for example it has no focus on wisdom or any intention to educate. In fact the Song of Songs is a collection of erotic poetry, quite like other love poetry from the Ancient Near East but it remains an unusual book no matter how you try to describe it.

Although the majority of books in the wisdom tradition come from the post-exilic period (ranging between about the fifth century and the second century BC), Proverbs seems to contain earlier material. Some would trace this back to Solomon himself, whereas others are more hesitant about whether Proverbs contains writing that is that old.

Visionary material

FOUND IN: Daniel and Revelation (with other books containing chapters or passages of visionary material)

OUTLINE: revelation of the secrets of heaven

POSSIBLE DATES OF COMPOSITION: Daniel, probably c.200; Revelation c.90s AD

The only category of material that spans both the Old and the New Testaments is the visionary material that scholars often call Jewish Apocalyptic literature (the word apocalyptic comes from the Greek word for Revelation and so means simply revelatory material). In the Old Testament this can be found in the book of Daniel (which despite its position in the Christian Old Testament is not really prophecy in the way the other prophetic books are) and in the New Testament in the book of Revelation. As well as these more book-length apocalypses, there are shorter chapters in other books like Isaiah 24–7, Zechariah 12–14, Mark 13 and Matthew 24.

The purpose of apocalyptic literature is to reveal the hidden secrets of God, either by angels descending to earth or by human beings looking into heaven or even ascending there themselves. In the course of this, the human beings often have, what are to our mind, weird visions involving beasts, dragons and angels involved in full-scale warfare. While many modern readers find this kind of material so alien that they often avoid it entirely, this was a very common form of writing between about the third century BC and the fourth century AD.

The book of Daniel, although set in the sixth century BC during the Babylonian exile, is widely thought, due to various errors and unusual historical detail, to have been written during the Greek period of the second century. The book of Revelation probably comes from the late first century AD.

The Gospels

FOUND IN: Matthew, Mark, Luke and John

OUTLINE: accounts designed to communicate the good news of Jesus Christ

POSSIBLE DATES OF COMPOSITION: late 60s AD to 90s AD

When we enter the Christian New Testament, we begin to encounter a different type of writing. The Gospels (Matthew, Mark, Luke and John) tell the story not of a whole nation but of the life of one man: Jesus of Nazareth. The word gospel comes from the Old English word *god-spell* and means good news. This is an excellent description of what the authors of the Gospels thought they were writing, because each one of them makes clear that what they think they are writing is not just any old historical account but something that will be good news to those who read it. There has been a lot of discussion about what kind of books the gospels are but many today would accept that they are a kind of biography in the style of a good number of other biographies in the Graeco-Roman period.

The first three gospels, Matthew, Mark and Luke, tell their story in a similar (though certainly not identical) way. Indeed in a good number of parts of the gospels, the accounts given by Matthew, Mark and Luke agree almost word for word. As a result these three are often called the synoptic gospels, since the word synopsis comes from a Greek word meaning to look together. Over the years many theories have been proposed about why it is that Matthew, Mark and Luke have such similar accounts of Jesus' life. The solution often suggested by scholars is that they either copied one another, or used a hypothetical common source (called by scholars 'Q'), or both.

John's Gospel is markedly different from the other three. The gospel has events in different orders, a number of different accounts, and, most strikingly of all, extensive reflections on the significance of what Jesus said.

As with many issues affecting the study of the Bible, there are a wide range of views about when the gospels were written but most scholars today would accept that they reached their final form sometime between the late 60s and early 90s AD with Mark probably written first (in the late 60s or early 70s), followed by Matthew (in the early 70s), Luke (in the late 70s or possibly early 80s) and John (in the early 90s).

To this brief examination of the gospels we also need to add the Acts of the Apostles. Unlike the other gospel writers, the author of Luke's Gospel did not finish the 'good news' with the resurrection of Jesus but, instead, continued it to demonstrate how it spread from Jerusalem to Rome. The first ten chapters of Acts focus on the twelve apostles, particularly Peter, and what happened to the earliest Jewish followers of Jesus after Jesus' ascension but from there its attention widens to the Gentile world and to the activities of Paul, who after initially persecuting the followers of Jesus became one of the early Christians' greatest missionaries.

Some scholars have attempted to argue that Luke-Acts is to be treated as a single book but there is little evidence to support this, not least the presence of a prologue at the beginning of both Luke and Acts. Nevertheless Acts is a vital part of the story and, while not a gospel as such, because apart from anything else it is not a biography of a single person, most certainly sits alongside the gospels in terms of what it was trying to communicate. There is much discussion about its date but many would place it slightly after the gospel of Luke so probably in the late 70s or early 80s, though others argue for an early 60s date and others still push it into the second century AD.

The letters

FOUND IN: Romans, 1 and 2 Corinthians, Galatians, Ephesians, Philippians, Colossians, 1 and 2 Thessalonians, 1 and 2 Timothy, Titus, Philemon, James, 1 and 2 Peter, 1, 2 and 3 John, Jude

OUTLINE: letters to communities and individuals among the earliest Christians

POSSIBLE DATES OF COMPOSITION: c. early 50s–90s AD

The other major type of material in the New Testament is letters. The majority of these are from St Paul to the communities he founded across Asia Minor and Greece. In a few of Paul's letters he commends the communities for their faith and faithfulness (e.g. 1 Thessalonians) but most are written to correct errors of judgement, teaching or practice in the years that followed. The letters of Paul have been particularly significant in helping to shape Christian belief and practice since so much of what he wrote is concerned with reflecting on what difference Christ's death, resurrection and ascension make to the lives of those who follow him.

The Pauline epistles were written to communities and addressed the issues that arose in these communities. In recent years, however, the Pauline authorship of some of these letters has been questioned by scholars. The so called Pastoral Epistles (1 and 2 Timothy and Titus) which are addressed to individuals rather than a group and the more church-focused Ephesians and Colossians have all had their Pauline authorship queried on the grounds both of the language used within them and the ideas they discuss. This is, however, an on-going debate about which there is little consensus by scholars.

The other epistles are normally gathered under the title of the Catholic Epistles. In this instance the word catholic means cyclical or universal and refers to the fact that, unlike with the Pauline epistles, their names refer not to the recipients but the traditional author of the epistle. As a result the epistles are not designed for one group or individual but for a range of people. In reality only five of the Catholic Epistles deserve this title since 2 and 3 John are clearly addressed to individuals. Recent years has seen extensive questioning of the authorship of each of these epistles, with some scholars doubting whether the names of the epistles have any connection with their authors.

Miscellaneous

All libraries contain books which defy categorization. The Bible is no different. Just a few books are very hard to put into categories largely because they are so very different from the rest of the books. In the Old Testament the books of Ruth and Esther fall into this category. Both are unusual stories about brave women who resisted the events that threatened them in order to live a better life. Another feature that makes them unusual is that in the book of Ruth, God is mentioned rarely, whereas in the book of Esther God is not mentioned at all.

Another Old Testament book that defies categorization is Lamentations. Some call it wisdom literature (though it does not bear much resemblance to any other wisdom text, with the possible exception of Job), whereas others take seriously its supposed authorship by Jeremiah and treat it as a prophetic text. In reality it is hard to categorize and contains moving poetic laments about the fall of Jerusalem to the Babylonians.

In some ways the book of Genesis (and the first half of Exodus) also falls into the hard to categorize section. Although in both the Jewish and Christian collections it is placed alongside law, it is clearly not law as the other texts are. At the same time, the history it contains is different from the historical books because it refers to a period long before the settlement in the land, and also has more than its fair share of talking animals. As a result it may have to stay in the hard to categorize section since it doesn't quite fit elsewhere.

In the New Testament, the book which is hardest to place in a category is the book of Hebrews. For many years, from the fourth century onwards, Hebrews was regarded as another of Paul's epistles. This is now widely discounted, not least because, unlike the other Pauline letters, Hebrews makes no claim in the book as to its own authorship. Indeed one of the striking features of the book of Hebrews is that it doesn't look like any of the other epistles in the New Testament. Indeed many scholars today would call it not an epistle but a sermon, since it bears many more of the hallmarks of a homily than it does an epistle.

The sixty-six volumes that make up the collection we call the Bible are different in style, content and date. They range from law books to poetry, from biography to letters, from wise sayings to visions. Although there are times when more books were written or reached their final form (particularly the sixth–fifth centuries and the latter half of the first century), the books were written over the span of around a thousand years. As a result, picking up the Bible at Genesis and attempting to read it as though it were a novel written by a single hand raises all sorts of problems for understanding it and what it is trying to say. The Bible is best treated as a library with the recognition that some books will be easier to read and more apparently relevant than others. This doesn't mean that we shouldn't try, for example, to read the law books; simply that these might not be the best books to begin with. It also means that it is worth working out what kind of book we are about to read before beginning; this will make it much easier to work out what is going on in the book and why.

3
Canon

Many conspiracy theories about the origins of the early Church have as one of their key ingredients a suspicion about how the decision was made about which books were to be treated as sacred Scripture (i.e. canonical) and which books were not. It is very easy to imagine all sorts of nefarious reasons for the inclusion of some books and the exclusion of others. There have been many arguments, some scholarly, and a lot less so, that claim that groups or individuals chose certain books for the canon in order to eradicate some strands of early Christianity or to introduce new ideas into the Christian tradition. In reality, the facts are much less exciting than this. The canons of both testaments emerged slowly over time largely due not to the malign influence of one or more individuals, but to a growing consensus among those who used them that the books included were to be treated as essential for life and worship. The development of each testament (Old and New) has a different story and so we will need to look at them one by one.

The word canon comes from a Greek word which means a reed, rule or measuring stick. In the Graeco-Roman world the word came to be used to describe the principle by which something could be judged. Among the early Christians of around the fourth century it began to be used as a way of describing the decrees of their early councils, and slowly began to be used to describe books recognized by the Church as Scripture. One of the challenges of writing about the development of the canon is that the word 'canon' was not used in the early period to describe an authorized collection of books, yet it is the word most commonly used today to mean this. As a result, although I will use the word canon to describe an authorized list of books, I do so some-what hesitantly in the knowledge that no early writer – Christian or otherwise – would have used the word in the way we do now.

What is canonical and what is not?

The Old Testament Apocrypha/ deuterocanonical literature

Although Jewish tradition only has twenty-four books in the Tanakh to the Christian thirty-nine in the Old Testament, they are, in fact, the same books, since Jewish tradition counts the books of Samuel as a single volume and likewise the books of Kings, Chronicles, Ezra-Nehemiah, and the twelve Minor Prophets. This makes twenty-four in all, in contrast to Christian tradition which itemizes them all separately getting to thirty-nine, which, added to the twenty-seven books of the New Testament, makes a total Christian canon of sixty-six books.

Within the Christian tradition, there are, in addition to the thirty-nine widely accepted books of the Old Testament, some additional books which are considered to be canonical by the Eastern Orthodox and Roman Catholic Churches, though not by Protestant Churches. These additional books are found in the Septuagint (the Greek translation of the Hebrew Scriptures; on this see more below) but not in the Hebrew Scriptures.

These books were widely used by many, though not all, Christians until the time of the Reformation, but then were rejected by the Protestant Reformers who only considered the books that were in the Hebrew Scriptures canonical. The Council of Trent, an Ecumenical council of the Roman Catholic Church which met in 1545 to reflect on the challenges posed by the Protestant Reformation, argued vehemently against this view and declared the additional books to be canonical. Indeed the

Council of Trent developed the term 'deuterocanonical' for these books to indicate that they related closely to the proto-canonical books (by which they meant the books of the Hebrew Scriptures) but were simply written later.

These deuterocanonical books include:

- Tobit
- Judith
- Additions to the book of Esther (10.4–16.24)
- The Wisdom of Solomon
- Sirach (also known as Ben Sira or Ecclesiasticus)
- Baruch
- Additions to Daniel (which include the Prayer of Azariah 3.24–90, Susannah 13 and Bel and the Dragon 14)
- 1 and 2 Maccabees

Eastern Orthodox Churches also call the additional books deuterocanonical but they mean something different by the term. The Roman Catholic Church uses the term 'deuterocanonical' to mean that the books are of equal authority but compiled later than the Hebrew Scriptures. In contrast the Eastern Orthodox Churches often use the phrase to mean books that should be read in services but which are of secondary authority to the protocanonical books, or Hebrew Scriptures. Their deuterocanonical books also contain additional material such as 3 Maccabees and 1 Esdras. Alongside the deuterocanonical books, various Eastern Orthodox Churches also view texts, like Psalm 151 and the Prayer of Manasseh, as of some value or, like 4 Maccabees and 2 Esdras, worthy of being included in an appendix.

The Protestant Reformers, and indeed the majority of Protestant Christians today, continue to regard the deuterocanonical books as un-canonical and call them apocryphal texts, or the Apocrypha. Indeed one of the biggest differences between a Roman Catholic translation of the Bible and a Protestant translation is the placing and/or inclusion of these books. In Roman Catholic translations (like the New Jerusalem Bible) these books and additions are to be found interwoven with the Hebrew texts. So, for example, the additions to Daniel are found at the chapter and verse numbers given after the name. In Protestant translations the books are either omitted entirely (e.g. the New International Version – NIV – has no Apocrypha at all) or bound in together between the Old and New Testaments (e.g. the New Revised Standard Version – NRSV – often has the Apocrypha as a separate section after the Old Testament).

The content of the Apocrypha can vary from translation to translation. The King James Version (KJV), published in the seventeenth century, contained all the books from the Roman Catholic deuterocanonical material with the addition of 1 and 2 Esdras. Many modern versions of the Apocrypha follow this but others also include 3 and 4 Maccabees and Psalm 151 in the Apocrypha.

The word Apocrypha or apocryphal means simply 'those things that are hidden' but became used in the Reformation of the sixteenth century in such a negative way that the word is now popularly used for something which is unreliable. So an apocryphal story is one which is widely told but believed to be untrue.

The apocryphal New Testament

One of the most confusing elements of this area is the fact that as well as an apocryphal Old Testament, there is also what is called an apocryphal New Testament. It is very important not to confuse the two. The Apocrypha or deuterocanonical material of the Old Testament is in many ways similar in style and content to the Old Testament itself. In fact, many people, when presented with one passage from undisputed canonical Old Testament and one from the Apocrypha/deuterocanonical literature, struggle to work out which is which. In addition it was also commonly said for many years that the Apocrypha/deuterocanonical literature was less reliable because it was only written in Greek and not in Aramaic or Hebrew. Even this view is now changing with the recognition that many of these books, although now only preserved in Greek, were originally written in Aramaic or Hebrew and only later translated into Greek. The major differences between the Apocrypha/deuterocanonical literature and the Hebrew Bible are that they were written later than the books of the Hebrew Scriptures and, most crucially of all, not accepted into the Hebrew canon of Scripture.

In great contrast the apocryphal New Testament (or New Testament Apocrypha) contains some texts which are very, very different in both style and content to that of the New Testament, as well as other texts which are not so different but which are thought by most scholars to have been written later than the New Testament. Most important of all is the fact that there is no 'official' New Testament Apocrypha and different collections contain different texts. So for example one of the major editions of the New Testament Apocrypha does not contain Gnostic texts (J. K. Elliott (ed.) *The Apocryphal New Testament: A Collection of Apocryphal Christian Literature in an English Translation*. OUP, Oxford, 2005), whereas the other major collection does (W. Schneemelcher (ed.) *New Testament Apocrypha, Revised Edition*, Westminster John Knox Press, Louisville, 2003).

THE GNOSTIC GOSPELS

Gnostic gospels of various kinds have, over the years, caused a great stir in the popular imagination. Gnosticism is the label given by twentieth- and twenty-first-century scholars to a widespread pattern of thought which can be found not only in Christianity but also in Judaism, Zoroastrianism and Graeco-Roman Mystery Religions. Although there are many different forms of Gnosticism, what connects them all is a belief that the material world is evil and that freedom from this material world can only be achieved through knowledge (the Greek word for knowledge is *gnosis*, hence the label Gnosticism).

The Gnostic gospels are an eclectic collection found at different times throughout the twentieth century. The most famous discovery occurred at Nag Hammadi in Egypt in 1945, shortly before the discovery of the Dead Sea Scrolls at Qumran (for more on the Dead Sea Scrolls see the text box on p. 75). Two Egyptian brothers found twelve leather-bound papyrus codices (or book-style manuscripts of papyrus held together between a binding as opposed, in this period, to the more common scrolls) while digging for fertilizer. These codices were found to contain a range of Gnostic texts written in Coptic, some of which were in the form of gospels. The most famous of these gospels is the Gospel of Thomas which contains sayings by Jesus (though no account of his life), many of which overlap with sayings in the canonical gospels. Most recent among such gospels to receive widespread attention has been the Gospel of Judas and the Gospel of Jesus' wife, though this latter text has subsequently been considered to be fraudulent.

Many people are intrigued by the Gnostic gospels and they are held up by some as representing an authentic position in early Christianity, a position that was later squashed by the Church hierarchy. This has been encouraged by various popular supporters of the gospels in novels like *The Da Vinci Code* by Dan Brown. There is little evidence, however, that these texts had a widespread following in early Christianity, and they are more likely to represent the view of small sectarian groups.

In fact there is a wide variety of material included in New Testament Apocrypha and some books are much more important than others. The most important books include:

- The Gospel of Thomas, a gospel which is largely made up of sayings, which some, though certainly not all, scholars think might have been used by the canonical gospel writers as a source.

- The First Epistle of Clement, one of the earliest non-canonical books of the early Christian community, is dated to the late first or early second century AD. It is written by Pope Clement I to the community in Corinth in response to a dispute about some presbyters being deposed.
- The Didache is also very early, dated to the late first or early second century AD, and contains three major sections which explore Christian ethics, early Christian worship (particularly baptism and the Eucharist), and the important of Church organization.
- The Shepherd of Hermas, which is dated to somewhere in the first–second centuries, contains five visions which Hermas, a former slave, saw, followed by twelve commandments and ten parables.

The other books include a variety of works that can be categorized as:

- Gospels: two of the most striking types are the infancy gospels which tell fantastic (in both senses of the word) stories about Jesus' early life, and Passions which talk much more about Jesus' death.
- Acts: these are a variety of accounts which give more detail about the subsequent lives of the apostles.
- Epistles: a number of letters between individuals and/or communities which discuss some of the key issues for the early Christian community. Particularly interesting is the third epistle to the Corinthians which purports to continue the dialogue between Paul and the Corinthians Church.
- Apocalypses: these contain accounts of visions which various people had.

There is also a range of other texts.

The Pseudepigrapha

Some other texts are worth mentioning here because they are sometimes referred to as a collection and can cause confusion. The word pseudepigrapha means literally 'false name' and, if technically used, refers to texts which claim to be by one person but were really written by another. There are some scholars who would claim that the vast majority of the Bible is pseudepigraphical on the grounds, they argue, that Moses did not write the Torah, nor David the Psalms, nor Jeremiah Lamentations, nor Matthew the gospel of that name, nor Paul 1 Timothy (and so on). Others at the other end of this particular spectrum of opinion would dispute some or all of these points and argue, for example, that Paul did write 1 Timothy.

Although these discussions continue, when the phrase Old Testament Pseudepigrapha is used it is not used to refer to texts from the Old Testament that claim to be written by one author but were written by another. The Old Testament Pseudepigrapha, though having no formal status at all, is a collection of texts which scholars have deemed to be important as texts that can be read alongside, and so illuminate, the Bible. The phrase 'the Old Testament Pseudepigrapha' was used by R.H. Charles to describe the texts which he gathered together and published in 1912 under the title *The Apocrypha and Pseudepigrapha of the Old Testament*. This collection contained texts most of which were thought to have been written between the second century BC and the second century AD. In 1972 James H. Charlesworth was commissioned to update Charles' work both in terms of new translations and of what was included in the collection. This was published in 1983 and continues to be widely used among scholars but has no official status in either Judaism or Christianity. They are texts gathered together for interest's sake and nothing more.

The formation of the canon of the Hebrew Scriptures

In the previous chapter we noticed that the Hebrew Scriptures are split into three main collections – Torah (or law); Prophets (in Hebrew Nevi'im); and Writings (in Hebrew Ketuvim) – and is, as a result, often called the Tanakh, a name derived from the first letter of each of these collections. This name, however, only began to be used for the whole collection of the Hebrew Scriptures at a relatively late date (*c.* fifth–sixth century AD). Before then the early Jewish name for the Scriptures was *Mikra* which means 'what is read', referring to the fact that these books were read during worship.

This alerts us to the importance of reading out loud in the history of the Bible. There can be no doubt that the reading of texts was important from an early point in Israel's history, and that what was read was considered to be sacred and authoritative. Even in the book of Exodus, Moses is recorded as reading from the book of the Covenant in such a way as lends what he said an authority: 'Then he took the book of the covenant, and read it in the hearing of the people; and they said, "All that the LORD has spoken we will do, and we will be obedient"' (Exodus 24.7). In fact the book of the Covenant is thought now to be a part of the book of Exodus itself (Exodus 20.22–33.33). Later on the book of the law is said to have been found in the Temple and read to King Josiah; it shaped the reforms he then enacted in Judah (2 King 22.8–11). Even if we recognize that the reports which record these occasions of reading out loud were written after the event, the recognition of the importance of reading out loud can be seen to be embedded firmly into the history of Israel.

This theme is picked up again when the people returned from Exile and Ezra read out the law to the people. The description of the reading out of the law, which is given in Nehemiah 8, implies that what Ezra read out was some kind of combination of Leviticus and Deuteronomy. This suggests that the Torah was taking shape in this period, and may even have looked quite like our Torah today, certainly containing parts of Leviticus and Deuteronomy and maybe other texts as well.

For many years, scholars believed that the evidence of Nehemiah pointed to the Torah reaching its final form in around 400 BC, and that the other two collections were finalized subsequently: the Prophets in around 200 BC and the Writings around 100 AD. In reality this schema is probably too neat and is increasingly criticized and abandoned by scholars today. The evidence seems to suggest a process that is much less clear and formal than this, and which remained fluid for a very long time.

One of the earliest references to texts which we would now consider biblical can be found in the second century BC when there began to be references in various texts to the Law and the Prophets. So for example, the second-century text Sirach (also called Ecclesiasticus or Ben Sira) mentions in its prologue 'the Law and the Prophets and the others that followed them' or 'the Law and the Prophets and the other books of our ancestors'. Also significant is the fact that there is a recitation of historical figures in chapters 44–50 of Sirach which mentions characters in the order that we now have them in the Hebrew Scriptures and which go as far as Nehemiah (a book which is to be found in the Writings). The problem is that the reference is somewhat vague and it is not easy to tell which books are meant by the headings of Law or Prophets. Philo, writing in the early first century AD, is similarly ambiguous, since he refers to the 'laws and oracles delivered through the mouth of prophets, and psalms …' and states that they (i.e. the Jews) 'read the holy writings and seek wisdom from their ancestral philosophy' (in *Vita Contemplativa* 25 and 28).

Intriguingly there are similar kinds of references in the New Testament, since on numerous occasions Jesus is reported as referring to either the Law and the Prophets (Matthew 7.12, 11.13, 22.40, Luke 16.16, John 1.45) or to the Law, the Prophets and the Psalms (Luke 24.44). This last reference is particularly important. In the tripartite Hebrew Scriptures the Psalms are in the collection called the Writings. This may suggest that Jesus is referring here to two of the three collections in full and one in part. It is worth noting, however, that regular references are made in the gospels to the book of Daniel (which in the Hebrew Scriptures is in the Writings and not among the Prophets as in the Christian Old Testament). This seems to indicate that Daniel was also considered authoritative at the time of Jesus and may suggest either that it was treated as one of the prophets or that other parts of the Writings were also accepted at this time.

It is also worth recognizing that although the Hebrew order of the Law and the Prophets was pretty static (and always had been), the order of the books in the collection of Writings was not. As a result the Writings are found in different orders in different manuscripts (a good excuse if ever anyone challenges you to list the books of the Bible in order).

There is little agreement about when the Hebrew Scriptures reached a settled final form, though many scholars suggest it was around the second century AD. It is important to realize though that between about the second century BC and the second century AD the texts of the Hebrew Scriptures shifted and changed, and some versions of them – especially those that were translated into Greek – contained texts which are not now found in the Hebrew Scriptures.

The Septuagint

One of the most famous of these Greek translations is known as the Septuagint. The romantic legend recorded in the Letter of Aristeas about the translation of this text associates it with the Pharaoh Ptolemy II Philadelphus who is said to have commissioned seventy scholars to translate the Torah into Greek for his library in Alexandria. Philo of Alexandria expanded the legend to include the notion that the scholars were all isolated from each other while they translated the text but that when they returned they had all produced an identical translation. It will not come as much of a surprise to discover that few scholars today accept this theory of the translation of the Septuagint but the legend lingers on in the abbreviation for the translation which you will often see written as LXX (the Roman numerals for seventy).

There is extensive discussion about when the Septuagint might actually have been translated (rather than what the legend says about it) and many scholars today suggest that this took place over a long period of time between the third and first centuries BC. They also recognize that there is a high chance that it was not solely translated in Alexandria and that a good number of the books may have been translated into Greek in Palestine. The Septuagint was not the first Greek translation of the Hebrew Scriptures to have been made but it is the only extant complete translation of the Hebrew Scriptures into Greek. It is probably also worth knowing that the word 'Septuagint' is often not used technically and can often be used loosely not to refer to the actual translation of the Septuagint itself but to any translation of the Hebrew Scriptures into Greek.

The Septuagint differs from the Hebrew Scriptures both in small and in much bigger ways. One of the smaller differences is some of the words used. Some of these differences can be attributed simply to the act of translation or to the interpretation that inevitably takes place when you translate something, but other differences suggest that the Hebrew text used by the Greek translators was not the same Hebrew text as we now have available to us.

Of the bigger differences between the Septuagint and the Hebrew Scriptures two of the most important are that the Septuagint does not have a threefold partition of Torah, Prophets and Writings and that it contains more books than the Hebrew Scriptures.

Indeed there is no hint at all of a threefold collection within the Septuagint. This seems to suggest that the translators of the Septuagint either didn't know or didn't accept this threefold collection within the Hebrew Scriptures and decided to order the books in a different way. It was this order, rather than the Hebrew order, then, that was adopted by the Christian church, probably because the majority of Christians were Greek speakers rather than Hebrew speakers and so used the Septuagint in preference to the Hebrew Scriptures.

The other major difference relates to the additional books contained in the Septuagint but not found in the Hebrew Scriptures. These books comprise the contested material known as the Apocrypha/deuterocanonical literature mentioned above. The presence of these additional books suggests that between the third and first centuries BC (when the Septuagint was translated) there was little agreement about what was regarded as part of the Scriptures and what was not.

This impression is further reinforced by discoveries at Qumran and the texts known commonly as the Dead Sea Scrolls. All of the canonical books of the Bible were found at Qumran (with the exception of the book of Esther). Alongside the biblical books, however, were a wide range of other Jewish texts, some from what we would now call the Apocrypha (such as parts of Tobit or Ben Sirach) and some which are now collected only in the Pseudepigrapha. Particularly important at Qumran was the book of 1 Enoch which was found in ten different manuscripts among the Dead Sea Scrolls, indicating that it was treated with a high degree of reverence by the community.

The assumption for centuries has been that the Hebrew text was the earlier and that the Greek translation represented a deviation from the more original Hebrew. The versions of the books of the Bible found at Qumran suggest that this may not be the case. For example what was found of the books of 1 and 2 Samuel at Qumran indicated that the Greek translators were

THE DEAD SEA SCROLLS

The mid-twentieth century was a time of great archaeological discovery. In 1497, two years after the discovery of the texts at Nag Hammadi, some Bedouin shepherd boys were throwing stones into some high up, remote caves in a place called Khirbet Qumran. When they heard breaking pottery, they realized that something was in the caves. On further investigation, they discovered that the caves contained large numbers of pots in which scrolls and fragments of scrolls were stored. This discovery led to a huge archaeological investigation which discovered scrolls in eleven different caves with the remains of a settlement nearby, approximately one mile from the north-west shore of the Dead Sea.

There are many conflicting theories about who the people might have been who lived at Qumran but many scholars now agree that the Qumran community was a radical sectarian Jewish group with a strong interest in the end of the world and in God's intervention to change what they saw as a corrupt leadership. When the Romans began to win the Jewish war in 67–70 AD, it is thought that the community fled from Qumran and hid the scrolls in the caves to keep them safe until they returned, which they did not.

The scrolls found in the caves contain many different types of texts, from rules which affected how the community lived, to visionary texts which envisioned God's salvation of his people, to books of the Bible and interpretations of those books. The writings reveal a group of people who were passionate about their faith and about the Bible and determined to fight against those whom they perceived to be corrupt.

When the scrolls first began to be published many people wondered whether they might overturn everything we know about early Christianity. In reality the opposite has been the case. The Dead Sea Scrolls shed light on what it might have felt like to be Jewish in the first century, and by doing that also illuminate some of the key issues for the earliest Jewish Christians.

using a Hebrew text much closer to what was found at Qumran than what is in the later Hebrew Masoretic text. The Hebrew Masoretic text, which is what we now use as the basis for translations of the Hebrew Scriptures, was established by Rabbis (known as the Masoretes) in the medieval period and had always been assumed to be a faithful witness to the text of the Hebrew Scriptures in the first century. Add to this the fact that some of the books in the Apocrypha/deuterocanonical literature were also found at Qumran (most notably fragments of a Hebrew version of Sirach and an Aramaic translation of Tobit) and it becomes clear that these new findings begin to change our understanding of the nature of the canon of the Hebrew Scriptures. It throws into the air traditional assumptions about the reliability of the Hebrew version of the Scriptures and points to two key conclusions. The first is that the Hebrew Masoretic text itself may not be as faithful a witness to the text that might have been read in the first century as has been traditionally assumed and the other, that there is no finally agreed canon of Hebrew Scriptures in the first century.

This second point is very important, since it indicates that not only can we *not* be definite about which books were regarded as fixed in this period, but also that there may have been extensive fluidity about which communities used which books before the second century AD. One example of this is the New Testament book of Jude, which alludes to the story of the fallen angels that can be found in 1 Enoch without stopping to indicate what status of text 1 Enoch might be. Thus 1 Enoch was important, if not more than that, to the author of Jude, and 1 Enoch is a text which now has no official authoritative status at all.

The question that emerges from all of this evidence is why then did the rabbis begin to fix a final form of the canon around the second century AD, when before this it did not appear to be necessary? The answer to this seems to be Christians. The formation of the Hebrew canon seems to have been, at least in part, in reaction to the formation of a Christian canon of Scripture. Those books which appeared to be overtly Christian were rejected on these grounds.

The formation of the New Testament canon

The Scriptures of the New Testament writers

In contrast to the story of the formation of the Old Testament canon, the story of the formation of the New Testament is more straightforward, if a little lengthy.

The place to begin is with the word 'Scripture', since it is important to recognize that the New Testament writers did not think that they were writing 'Scripture'. Whenever the word Scripture is used in the New Testament it is referring backwards to the Old Testament (though of course they would not have thought of it as the Old Testament as there wasn't another Testament yet). This attitude to Scripture continued well into the second century AD so that some of the early Christian writers who wrote just after the New Testament (e.g. 1 Clement and the Shepherd of Hermas) used the word Scripture to refer to the Old Testament and only occasionally alluded to texts that we would now recognize as New Testament texts.

The New Testament writers wrote in Greek and quoted in Greek from the Old Testament. One of the intriguing features of their use of the Old Testament, though, is that they do not always quote from the Septuagint. There are some quotes which are clearly from the Septuagint: so for example in Matthew 21.16, Jesus is reported as saying 'Out of the mouths of infants and nursing babies you have prepared praise for yourself' which is what the Septuagint says, whereas the Masoretic Hebrew text says 'Out of the mouths of babes and infants you have founded a bulwark because of your foes' (Psalm 8.2) which even the most untrained eye can recognize to be very different. Elsewhere, however, the gospels quote from something that is much closer to our Hebrew text, so for example in Matthew 11.29 Jesus exhorts his hearers to 'Take my yoke upon you, and learn from me; for I am gentle and humble in heart, and you will find rest for your souls' which draws on the Hebrew of Jeremiah 6.16 that talks of finding rest for your souls, not, as the Septuagint has it, purification.

As we noticed when we were exploring the Septuagint, it is quite possible that there were different versions of both Hebrew and Greek texts of the Old Testament floating around at the time of Jesus and it is likely that the differences in the references to the Old Testament in the New Testament texts reflect this.

The writing of the New Testament

It is widely accepted that the earliest New Testament texts to be written were those of Paul's epistles which are commonly dated to the 50s and 60s AD. Paul's epistles are written either to Christian communities which he, Paul, founded (e.g. 1 and 2 Corinthians) or to those that he hadn't yet met but intended to meet soon (e.g. Romans). One of the intriguing features of Paul's epistles is that they address primarily theological and ethical issues (in other words who Jesus was and how Christians might live differently as a result). One subject they simply do not cover in any detail is the life and sayings of Jesus. Some think that this was because Paul had never met Jesus and so knew few of the stories about him; while others believe that he doesn't mention them simply because he assumes that everyone already knew them and didn't need them repeating.

These stories about Jesus' life and sayings are, instead, recorded in the gospel accounts. It is impossible here to look in detail at the different theories about how the gospels came to be written but a brief sketch of the major features might help. Many scholars believe that the earliest Christians told the stories of Jesus in oral form until eventually they began to be written down. When the gospel writers (particularly Matthew, Mark and Luke) began to write their gospels they used a written source (which many scholars call 'Q' after the German *Quelle* or source) and their own material to put together the gospels as we have them today. Often the gospel writers edited the material available to them so that it spoke particularly to the communities to whom they wrote. The three Synoptic Gospels, Matthew, Mark and Luke, are thought to date from somewhere between the late 60s and early 80s, whereas John's Gospel is more commonly dated to the early 90s AD. The other books of the New Testament have a spread of dates but most fall into the last three decades of the first century AD.

Towards a canon in the second and third centuries AD

One of the earliest people to refer to documents from what we now call the New Testament was Papias of Hierapolis whose own writings no longer survive but who is quoted by a later writer called Eusebius. Very little is known about him, apart from the claim by Irenaeus (a bishop in Gaul in the early second century) that Papias heard John the Apostle preach and was a friend of Polycarp (a bishop of Smyrna in the early second century AD). This little biographical information causes scholars to estimate that he lived from *c.*60 and *c.*135 AD.

Somewhat strikingly Papias is recorded as having said that 'I did not think that information from books would help me so much as the utterance of a living and surviving voice' (quoted in Eusebius *Church History*, III.xxxix.4). This illustrates that texts themselves were not particularly important to the earliest Christians and that they preferred where possible to hear the stories by word of mouth, even as late as the second century.

The shift towards the written word seems to coincide with the passing of a hundred years from Jesus' death when the gap between the events and the present became too long for any claim of reliable eyewitnesses.

Having said this, however, although he clearly preferred oral accounts, Papias mentioned the authorship of the Gospels of Mark and Matthew. From then on we can begin to see increasing references to books from the New Testament in the writings of early Christians: Polycarp, Papias' friend and bishop of Smyrna, mentions passages from the gospels, from Paul and from Hebrews and 1 Peter. It is important to recognize that at this point, in the mid-second century, there was no definitive list of books that formed the New Testament but there were references to books from what we now recognize as the New Testament and also collections of books found in the New Testament. Indeed Paul's epistles may have been treated as a collection as early as the end of the first century. This means that these books, particularly the gospels and the Pauline epistles, have begun a journey of increasing importance which eventually culminates in a fixed list of books, that we now call the canon of the New Testament.

Another key player along this journey was someone called Marcion of Sinope, who was a bishop in Asia Minor, and who around 130–140 AD seems to have been the first person to try and put together a clear list of books, in his view, that should form a New Testament. The problem was that Marcion held such extreme views that he was declared one of the first heretics by his fellow early Christians. Marcion held a number of views that troubled his early companions; for example he argued that Jesus did not really become a human being but just appeared to have a human body, but his most significant view, for our current exploration of the development of the canon, is that he thought that the God of the Old Testament was different from the God of the New Testament. The God of the Old Testament he viewed as being vindictive and angry and compared him with a God of the New Testament who was all loving and compassionate.

In order to achieve this view of the New Testament, Marcion needed to include some books and exclude others. As a result he was responsible for compiling what we might now call the first canon of the New Testament. Marcion's New Testament had two sections: the first contained a version of Luke's gospel and the second consisted of ten of Paul's epistles. All of these were edited, though, to reflect Marcion's view of a loving and compassionate New Testament God. Marcion's canon seems to have kick-started other Christians to propose which texts should be regarded as 'canonical'.

Shortly after Marcion's canon, Irenaeus, who was a bishop in Lugdunum in Gaul during the second century AD, argued vehemently in his work *Against Heresies* (3.11.7) in favour of four gospels (Matthew, Mark, Luke and John), and while doing so acknowledged that many Christians of his time either used only one gospel or more than four gospels. At a similar time, Tatian who was a Syrian Christian produced a harmonized gospel woven together from Matthew, Mark, Luke and John, known today as the *Diatessaron,* which was popular for many years among Syriac Christians. The *Diatessaron* attempted to smooth out contradictions in the narratives and omitted things like the genealogies in Matthew and Luke, where contradictions could not be smoothed out. The *Diatessaron* was never accepted outside of Syriac circles but illustrates that in the second century Christians were attempting to work towards a 'definitive' gospel about Jesus, which in the end could only be achieved by the inclusion of four gospels in the canon.

The earliest Orthodox list of books within the New Testament is called the Muratorian canon and is thought by most scholars to be dateable to about 170 AD (although it should be noted that a few scholars consider it to be much later and around the fourth century AD). The list of books is found on a fragment (known unsurprisingly enough as the Muratorian Fragment) and omits the names of the first two gospels but states that there are four gospels and contains the names of the second two, Luke and John (it is likely that the first two were Matthew and Mark since Irenaeus and Tatian viewed them alongside Luke and John as the central four but we cannot know for certain). The Muratorian Fragment also lists Acts and thirteen letters of Paul (i.e. Romans, 1 and 2 Corinthians, Galatians, Ephesians, Philippians, Colossians, 1 and 2 Thessalonians, 1 and 2 Timothy, Titus and Philemon) but not Hebrews which only later seems to have been regarded as written by Paul.

From the rest of the New Testament the fragment mentions Jude, two epistles by John (but not three as we now have them) and the Apocalypse of John (also known as Revelation). Intriguingly the Muratorian Fragment does not appear to link the John who wrote Revelation with the John who was the author of the gospel and epistles of John, although later this was a widely made connection. Also on the list is the Book of Wisdom (or Wisdom of Solomon), a text from the Septuagint which appears to have been popular in this period, and something called the Apocalypse of Peter which the fragment includes but advises against reading in church. Also in this category is the Shepherd of Hermas written in the late first–early second century, and widely read by early Christians.

The books which are simply not mentioned by the fragment include Hebrews, as mentioned above, 1 and 2 Peter, and James. Alongside these the fragment lists a number of texts which are explicitly excluded including two letters attributed to Paul but not by him (the letters to the Laodiceans and the Alexandrians) and a book of Psalms composed for Marcion.

Although lists were beginning to be made of acceptable (and unacceptable) books, the canon was far from fixed, and in the third century it is possible to observe quite a variety of views, including those of Origen (who was a scholar in Alexandria in

Egypt in the third century AD) who accepted the gospels and Pauline epistles, but expressed reservations about James, 2 Peter and 2 and 3 John.

Further developments in the fourth century AD

It was only in the fourth century that lists of biblical books became an important issue. Eusebius, who became bishop of Caesarea in 314 AD, gave a list of the undisputed books of the New Testament (which he gave as four gospels, the Acts of the Apostles, the epistles of Paul, the epistle of John, and the epistle of Peter, and then the Apocalypse of John if it seems proper). This inclusion of the Apocalypse of John indicates that Eusebius is ambivalent about the book; he is happy about its inclusion but suggests others are not. After this list Eusebius gave a list of books that are disputed – these include James, Jude, 2 Peter, 2 and 3 John and Hebrews. He also lists a number of books which should be explicitly excluded.

Later in the same century (*c*.367 AD) Athanasius who was a bishop in Alexandria gave a list of books in his Easter sermon that he termed 'canonized' (this is the closest the early Church came to using the word canon to describe this list of books). These included:

- a list of books of the Old Testament (in which there were twenty-two books, a number he reached by counting various books together as Jewish tradition does and excluding Esther);
- a list of books of the New Testament which included all twenty-seven of the books we now regard as being in the New Testament;
- a list of seven books that are not canonized but are worth reading which are the Wisdom of Solomon, the Wisdom of Sirach, Esther, Judith, Tobit, Didache and the Shepherd (of Hermas).

Also around this time Synods of the Church began to set down lists of New Testament books. 'Synod' is the particular word used for gatherings or councils of churches at which key decisions were made. In the early church these Synods were normally gatherings of bishops and their primary concern was to reach a consensus on what was 'orthodox' (i.e. what fitted within the accepted realm of Christian faith and, often more importantly, what fell outside of it). In *c*.363 (i.e. a similar time to Athanasius' Easter sermon) the Synod of Laodicea in Asia Minor stated that only canonical books were to be read in church but the original canons did not say which books these were. A later addition to these canons gives a twenty-two-book Old Testament (like Athanasius) and a twenty-six-book New Testament (i.e. it included Hebrews but omitted Revelation).

By the end of the fourth century, the lists of books in the canon become more and more consistent. Jerome (*c*.347–420), who was a priest and scholar of the church and who translated the Bible into Latin (normally called the Vulgate), used the twenty-seven books (including Revelation) that we now have in the New Testament, and was commissioned to carry out this translation by Pope Damasus I who gave a similar list of the books included in the canon. By the end of the fourth century, a consensus had emerged among Western Christians that the books of the Bible included what we would now recognize as the Old Testament (plus the deuterocanonical literature) and the New Testament.

The Eastern Churches, however, have always been more cir-cumspect about the concept of a canon and were much more open to books which are not formally included in the canon having spiritual value. It is also worth noting that although the majority of Eastern Orthodox Christians subsequently accepted the same twenty-seven books of the New Testament as Western Christians (following a council in Carthage *c*.387 AD), some parts of the Eastern Church never accepted the 'disputed' books. So, for example, the Peshitta which is the translation of the New Testament into Syriac (and hence the Scriptures of the churches in the Syriac tradition) originally excluded 2 Peter, 2 and 3 John, Jude and Revelation.

Martin Luther's canon

A fascinating post-script to all of this is that Martin Luther (1483–1546), who is widely accepted as the father of the Protestant Reformation, revived the concept of 'disputed' New Testament texts. For Luther there were four disputed New Testament books: Hebrews, James, Jude and Revelation. Luther argued vehemently that these should be excluded from the canon because of the ways in which he perceived them to contradict what he believed to be central New Testament doctrines (especially those of justification by faith alone). Ultimately Luther was unsuccessful in this attempt formally to exclude these books but they remain repositioned at the end of the New Testament in all Lutheran bibles (and in reality often unread in some Protestant circles).

The story of the formation of the New Testament canon reveals certain patterns which it is worth picking out of the detail of its development. The first is that Matthew, Mark, Luke and John were regarded relatively early (even as early as the mid-second century) as the four definitive gospels. The second is that the thirteen Pauline epistles (excluding Hebrews) were also recognized as being significant for Christians as a whole, again from the mid-second century. The other books have a more chequered career and were disputed longer until finally in the fourth century they became accepted as the twenty-seven books we now call the New Testament.

Contrary to popular conspiracy theories about the canon, it was not the work of a few powerful men but was the result of four centuries of use in public worship. The formation of the New Testament canon is probably the closest that it is possible to get to a wide consensus of what should and should not be included in a list.

The authority of the Bible

We cannot leave the question of the canon of the Bible without a brief exploration of what the canon of Scripture meant in terms of how the books were treated. The language normally used within the Christian tradition to refer to this is 'the authority of Scripture'. This phrase is used to refer to the belief that the Bible should be seen as being authoritative in matters of what humans think and do. Although Scripture has always, within the Christian tradition, been regarded as supremely authoritative, this is an issue which came to the fore particularly at the Protestant Reformation and formed one of the central pillars of subsequent Protestant belief.

The authority of the Hebrew Scriptures in early Judaism

One of the challenges of asking a question about the authority of the Bible in Judaism is that we need to begin by acknowledging the point made above which is that the whole area of scriptural authority is a primary concern of the Christian Protestant Reformation. As a result, asking the question within Judaism involves imposing onto Judaism something which is not theirs in the first place. The question of the authority of Scripture is simply not a question that is important within the Jewish tradition.

Having said this however, there are things to learn from a Jewish attitude to Scripture and two things in particular stand out.

The first relates to the text itself. When the Hebrew Scriptures are read out loud one of the issues to be borne in mind is the difference between the *qere* and *ketiv* form of the text. *Qere* means what is read and *ketiv* what is written. What this means is that the text is treated as sacred so that if any minor (or indeed major) error has been spotted over the years the text itself is not altered. Instead marginal notes are inserted alongside the relevant verse with the instruction to read out loud the corrected marginal form rather than the original written form. Sometimes the difference between the *qere* and *ketiv* is very minor but other times it is much greater. What is significant is that the inclusion of *both* the *qere* and the *ketiv* are considered important. So the text itself is maintained as it has been received, but is altered in what is read out loud.

A second issue is that Scripture is not deemed to be authoritative by itself but it is Scripture when interpreted by the rabbis. Thus within Judaism, Rabbinic interpretation of the Torah is as important as the Scripture itself. Alongside this is a view of a gradation of importance with the Torah being the most important followed by the Prophets and then the Writings.

The authority of the Bible from the early Church to the Reformation

In a sense one of the major issues for the early Church was the issue of authority, and in particular who could decide which views were 'orthodox' (i.e. in line with Christian belief) and which were 'heterodox' or 'heresy' (i.e. not in line with Christian belief). Indeed part of the reason for the formation of a Christian canon was that it provided the means of measuring what was orthodox and what was not.

In the second century, then, the question focused around which texts could be used to describe what Christians believed (hence Marcion's attempt to rule out the Old Testament as he attempted to define Christian faith in a particular way). By the time the canon was more fixed in the fourth century attention shifted away from what was authoritative, since that was settled as those texts in the canon, to working out what these texts meant. So the next big question became a question of method, in other words how to work out what the Bible was saying

Christian and Rabbinic Jewish practice here had much in common. In Judaism the rabbis became the central interpreters of Scripture; in Christianity the early Fathers were regarded in a similar light. Thus the key to understanding the Bible was seen to be the early Church Fathers writing from the second to the fifth centuries. Out of this grew a strong sense of the importance of Christian tradition which by the time of the Middle Ages was regarded by many writers as effectively the same thing as what the Church Fathers had said. So important was the Bible in the Middle Ages that it shaped much of society in the West, from the significance of the king to the nature of law, from language to economics. The Bible, as interpreted through Church tradition, was seen as the single authoritative source of what society was and should look like.

The authority of the Bible and the Protestant Reformation

Probably the biggest revolution in attitudes to the authority of Scripture came with the Protestant Reformation. The Reformers were hugely influenced by the Renaissance and in particular by the desire to go back to the Greek and Latin origins of society. One of the great cries of the time was 'ad fontes' which meant 'to the sources'. In terms of Christian thinking this meant returning to the Bible itself and reading it afresh apart from the influence of Church tradition.

This was accompanied by access, for the first time, to Greek versions of the Old and New Testaments (rather than the Latin translation which had dominated the study of the Bible up to this point in history) so that it felt possible for the first time to return to the very roots of Christianity and to see it with fresh eyes. Indeed one of the great principles of the Reformation was that every Christian ought to be able to read the Bible for themselves and to shape their own lives according to what they read. As a result one of the great works of the Reformation was the translation of the Bible from original languages into the 'vernacular' (i.e. the languages people actually spoke rather than ecclesiastical Latin).

Both Martin Luther and John Calvin saw the Bible as a supremely authoritative guide for what to believe and how to live. Both thought that all Christian doctrine and practice should be drawn exclusively from the Bible. In the generations that followed the Reformation these ideas were honed further. In the seventeenth century, in particular, the idea of biblical inspiration became particularly important. This is the idea that the Bible was directly inspired by God himself and as a result shared God's characteristics, of which the most important was truthfulness or inerrancy.

This view significantly changed the authority that Scripture was seen to hold. The Roman Catholic view was that the authority of Scripture was given to it by the Church's declaration that a book was part of the canon of Scripture; the reformers believed that the authority of Scripture came from divine inspiration. As a result, it was authoritative because it was God's word, not because the Church declared that it was. This view led to the concern to establish as accurate a version of the Bible as possible. If it contained God's words, then there was a great need to remove errors that might have crept in when scribes copied the text or when it was translated from one language to another.

The authority of the Bible and the Enlightenment

The next big stage in the whole question of the authority of the Bible is the period of Enlightenment which was a movement that sought to use reason with the goal that by doing so society would progress and develop. This movement inevitably began to raise questions about some elements of belief about the authority of the Bible. One of the key voices in this era was David Hume (1711–76) whose 'Essay on Miracles' questioned whether miracles could have happened because they went against the laws of nature. Following this, there was an increased interest in studying the Bible using the best possible reason and critical apparatus. As a result, extensive study began on the provability – or otherwise – of the historical events in the Bible and who might have written the books, when and how (often this led to views that the named author did not write them nor were they written when people traditionally believed that they were).

This critical evaluation of the text, known as the historical critical method, was considered by some Christians as destructive of faith and of the authority of the Bible, whereas for other Christians it was regarded as enhancing faith since it gave a proper rational underpinning for what people believed. In many ways the debate between the reformers' view of the inspiration of Scripture and the Enlightenment's view of the importance of rational, critical scriptural study continues. There are still those who argue for the inerrancy of Scripture on the one hand and still, on the other, those whose primary method of reading the Bible involves solely rational enquiry with little if any acknowledgement of the Bible's authority.

Many Christians today, however, would take some position between these two views and, while acknowledging the importance of critical study, would maintain that the Bible is still inspired. Scholars such as Karl Barth in the twentieth century proposed the view that while the Bible is 'the word of God' it is not 'the words of God'. Christians who follow this view believe that God can speak through the pages of the Bible but the actual words themselves are not inspired by God. Thus the phrase 'biblical inspiration' means as much that the Bible inspires its readers as it does that the Bible is inspired by God.

As is so often the case, the history of the development of the canon of Scripture is much more mundane than conspiracy theories about it. The development of the canon of both the Hebrew Scriptures and the New Testament was a long, consensual process, which in both cases was jolted into reaching a final form largely in reaction against certain views. So the Hebrew canon seems to have reached a final form in reaction to Christians and their use of the Scriptures; and the New Testament canon reached its final form in reaction to people like Marcion and their use of the Scriptures. In both the Hebrew Scriptures and the New Testament we can see that there are both core parts of the canon and less important parts. So in the Hebrew Scriptures the Torah is core, followed by the Prophets; the Writings, though still significant, are less important than the other two. In the New Testament the gospels and the Pauline epistles are core, and the other books have been the subject of more dispute.

4

Translation

Many people who have a little familiarity with the Bible will know it through the King James Version (KJV). This may be through the reading of the Bible in church and the stirring sonorous sound of, for example, John 1 read at Christmas Carol services: 'In the beginning was the Word, and the Word was with God, and the Word was God. The same was in the beginning with God. All things were made by him; and without him was not any thing made that was made. In him was life; and the life was the light of men' (John 1.1–4); or it may be through the many phrases that have made their way through from the KJV in to modern language like 'a law unto themselves' (from Romans 2.14) or 'a sign of the times' (from Matthew 16.3) or 'go the extra mile' (Matthew 5.41).

Indeed many people are so familiar with the KJV that it seems something of an affront to encounter the Bible in a different translation which can often sound wrong to people used to the KJV. As a result people often ask 'what is so wrong with the King James Version?' The quick answer is that there is absolutely nothing wrong with the KJV at all. It was a translation provided at a particular time, into a particular context, and as such was, and for many years remained, the best English translation available. The passing of time and, in particular, new archaeological discoveries and theories about translation have brought other translations into the market. This chapter will explore the different translations of the Bible, the principles that lie behind them, and the issues that translation raises for Bible reading.

Ancient Bible translations

Translation of the Bible is not new. Wherever the Bible has travelled to countries which do not speak the language in which it was originally written, it has been translated. It is hard to work out which translations of the Bible are earliest but two very early translations are translations into Aramaic and into Greek.

The Aramaic language originated from Aram, which was an ancient region in the centre of what is now Syria. The language probably began around the tenth century BC but became significant in the eighth century BC when it was widely used as the ordinary spoken language of the Assyrian empire. It continued as the common language (lingua franca) in the Babylonian and Persian empires and as a result became the lingua franca of Second Temple Judaism. Although Aramaic had different dialects, and even scripts, it was for many years spoken across the Ancient Near East. The impact of this was that Hebrew began to decline as a language until it was used solely for worship and in schools. As a result a translation was needed for most Jews when they heard the Scriptures read out in worship. Subsequent Jewish guidelines (in Mishnah Megillah 3.2) indicate that a translation was given orally from Hebrew into Aramaic, verse by verse for the Torah, and three verses by three verses for the Prophets. There was also a prohibition on writing the translation down. This prohibition eventually seems to have been overturned because there now exist some Aramaic translations of the Hebrew Bible, commonly called Targums (which simply means translations). Although the written Targums date from around the fourth century AD onwards, the tradition of translation into Aramaic may well have existed for the whole of the Second Temple period.

The other ancient translation, and one which in its written form predates the written Targums, is the translation into Greek. As we noted in the previous chapter (pp. 72–7), there were numerous translations of the Hebrew Scriptures into Greek but the most significant of all was the Septuagint (LXX). The LXX was probably translated over a period of around 200 years (between the third and first centuries BC) with the Torah being translated first and the rest of the books being included later. Later, in the second century AD there were at least three other Greek versions of the Bible produced: by Aquila, Symmachus and Theodotion, though there is little agreement about whether these are entirely fresh translations or improvements of the LXX. In the third century Origen put together in six columns the Hebrew Scriptures, a Greek transliteration of the Hebrew, the Septuagint, and these three translations so that they could be compared and contrasted. This is known as the Hexapla and unfortunately only exists in fragments today.

The Vulgate

Probably the most influential translation of the Bible in the whole of Church history was something known as the Vulgate. The Vulgate was largely, but not exclusively, the work of Jerome who was commissioned by Pope Damasus I (366–84 AD) to revise the existing Latin translations of the Gospels. Jerome did this first, but then moved onto other books. He translated the books of the Hebrew Scriptures from the Hebrew itself (with the exception of the Psalms which he translated from Origen's Hexapla; i.e. Greek and Hebrew); he translated some of the books of the Apocrypha/deuterocanonical literature variously from Theodotion's Greek translation, from the Septuagint, and from an Aramaic version. The Gospels, as mentioned above, were a revision of a previous Latin version in the light of the Greek text of the Gospels. Other parts of the Bible, including Paul's epistles and the book of Revelation, were probably translated by some other unknown people from a previous Latin translation.

This translation quickly became the definitive translation of the Bible in the Christian West and remained so until around 1530. This is not to say that there were no other translations, simply that there were no other translations as widely influential

and authorized as this one. In fact there were few Bible translations in the Middle Ages – not least because Bible translation was
discouraged in this period – but there are a few translations into
different languages, as well as a revision of the Vulgate.

ST JEROME

St Jerome was a priest in the early Church between c.347 and 420.
He was born Eusebius Sophronius Hieronymus in the Roman
province of Dalmatia (which is now the region in which countries
like Croatia, Serbia, and Bosnia and Herzegovina are to be found).
He went to Rome to study Greek. Following that he travelled first to
France and then to the Middle East, where he began to learn Hebrew.
He then returned to Rome and was ordained as a priest. The problem
was that he held what were considered to be such extreme views
that he made many enemies and eventually was forced to leave Rome.
At this point he returned to the Middle East and lived in Bethlehem.

He lived there in a hermit's cell, near the traditional site of
Jesus' birth, for around thirty-four years. Indeed visitors to the
Church of the Nativity in Bethlehem can, today, also visit Jerome's
cell where you can see graffiti left on the walls probably written by
scribes who worked for him. During this time he translated the
Bible and some of the books of the Apocrypha into Latin, working
with both the original Hebrew and Greek, as well as the Septuagint.

As well as this extensive translation work, Jerome also wrote a
large number of commentaries on the Bible as well as various
essays against heretics, though scholars do not consider most of
them to be very good.

Jerome died in Bethlehem in 420 AD.

Medieval and Reformation translations

Wycliffe's Bible

The most significant translations from the late medieval period
were those overseen by John Wycliffe (c.1330–84) but undertaken

by a number of different people translating the Bible from the
Vulgate into Middle English. The translations undertaken between
1382 and 1395 are now called Wycliffe's Bible (though there was
more than one of them). One of the reasons that lay behind the
translation was Wycliffe's belief that having the Scriptures in their
own language would help people to understand the gospel better.
Although these translations were hugely influential in the subsequent growth of Protestantism in England, the translations were
made from the Vulgate, included the Apocrypha, and fully
reflected Roman Catholic teaching. Nevertheless Wycliffe's Bible
was picked up and used extensively by adherents of Lollardy,
which was both a religious and political movement from the late
fourteenth to mid sixteenth centuries. The Lollards called vociferously for the reform of the Church. As a result Wycliffe's Bible
– and indeed English translations in general – became associated
with radical calls for reform and as a result was banned from use
in the early fifteenth century, though this did not seem to have
much impact upon its widespread popularity.

Wycliffe's Bible marks the beginning of a watershed in Bible
translation. Although he lived far too early to have been a part of
the Reformation himself, Wycliffe represented a passion for
allowing people to read the Bible in their own language and made
a significant critique of the Church. These two principles, among
others, became pillars of the subsequent Protestant Reformation.

Erasmus and the Greek New Testament

The next great figure in this narrative about the history of Bible
translation did not produce a translation himself, but worked on
the Greek text that many people used for subsequent translations.
Desiderius Erasmus (c.1466–1536) was a renaissance humanist.
Humanism was a movement which was passionate about education and in particular the ability to speak and write well. Erasmus
developed an interest in the Greek text of the Scriptures but,

though he sought to reform the Church, he always sought to do so from within instead of outside of it as the Reformers chose to do. Erasmus' Greek text of the New Testament, made possible by the Greek manuscripts which came to the West following the sack of Constantinople in 1453, for the first time in many centuries gave the opportunity for translators to engage with a text of the Bible that was not the Latin Vulgate.

This meant that it was possible to re-evaluate some of the phrases from the Vulgate on which various key doctrines had rested. Two of the most significant of these are Gabriel's greeting to Mary and the content of Jesus' message. The Vulgate's translation of Gabriel's greeting read 'Hail Mary, Full of Grace'. This had been understood to mean that Mary was a means by which grace was mediated to the world. Erasmus pointed out that the Greek didn't really say this; instead its meaning was more along the lines of 'accepted into grace' or 'favoured one'. The other key example, which was probably even more important, was what Jesus proclaimed in Matthew 4.17. The Vulgate's translation gave what Jesus said as 'Do penance for the Kingdom of Heaven is at hand' rather than, as Erasmus argued it should be translated, 'be penitent' or 'come to your senses' (in fact today the most common translation of this is 'repent'). It was these kinds of retranslations that gave space and underpinnings to many of the reformers' key theological arguments. What this alerts us to is the importance of translation in the formation of theology. It is easy to assume that Bible translation though necessary is not all that important. However, the shifts in meaning in certain verses of the New Testament that arose as a result of Erasmus' Greek versions of the New Testament illustrate that whole theological revolutions can arise from small changes in the translation of particular words.

All in all Erasmus produced five editions of the Greek New Testament in which he attempted to correct errors that had crept in through trying to finish the text too quickly. Some of these were simple printing errors, though others arose from using ancient manuscripts in which some key verses were omitted. These different versions of the Greek New Testament continued to be edited after Erasmus' death first by Theodore Beza (1519–1605) and then by Bonaventura Elzevir (1583–1652). Eventually in a preface to the 1633 edition of the text, the version was given the name Textus Receptus or received text. This became the major text used to translate the New Testament for the next 250 years.

English translations before the King James Version

Erasmus' Greek text gave rise to a flurry of new translations of the Bible including the Luther Bible (Martin Luther's translation of the Bible into German, 1534), a Polish Bible (1563), a French Bible (1530) and a Slovene Bible (1584). In England, following Wycliffe's Bible, the most important translator was William Tyndale. He became inspired by the need to translate the Bible into English but met severe opposition both in England and then elsewhere in Europe. The reasons for this opposition were many and complex but often arose out of a fear that heresy could arise if the Bible were read without the checks and balances provided by the Church authorities. He moved from place to place but was eventually executed in Antwerp in 1536. Before his death, however, Tyndale had translated the whole of the New Testament and part of the Old Testament. One of the most controversial of Tyndale's decisions was to avoid church language in his translation. Some key examples illustrate the impact of this decision: he used congregation instead of church, elder instead of priest, repent instead of do penance, and charity instead of love. His argument was that if an ordinary person was to understand the Bible, then it had to be translated into the language they spoke every day, not a special church language that they only heard in church services.

WILLIAM TYNDALE

William Tyndale was born in Gloucestershire in c.1494. He went to Magdalen Hall in Oxford (which later became Hertford College) as a teenager, though he also studied at Cambridge. Tyndale was a gifted linguist and swiftly learnt Latin, Greek, Hebrew, French, German, Italian and Spanish. During his studies, Tyndale clearly became influenced by the theology of the Reformers because in around 1522, he had various conflicts which seem to have focused around the Pope's authority. Also during this time, Tyndale appears to have been inspired by the work of Erasmus on the Greek text of the New Testament and to have developed a passion for the good translation of Scripture.

He attempted to find support in England for his translation of the Scriptures but by 1523 it became clear that he would not find the support he needed in England. So, in c.1524 he left and lived in Germany. During this time, he completed the first edition of his translation of the New Testament into English, and in 1529 as well as revising the New Testament began work on translating the Old Testament into English. His translations were published and were brought to England and became very popular, despite numerous attempts to stamp out their use.

Tyndale deeply opposed Henry VIII's divorce from Catherine of Aragon and wrote extensively stating his opinions on the matter. This almost certainly brought about his downfall and, although he never returned to England, he was hunted and eventually betrayed and captured in Antwerp in 1535. He was condemned to be strangled to death at the stake and his body subsequently burned. Tyndale 's last words are said to have been 'O Lord, Open the King of England's eyes'.

One of the sad ironies of Tyndale's story is that within four years of his death the Great Bible was published and was based almost entirely on Tyndale's translation.

Although Tyndale's Bible was banned, it continued to circulate secretly but already things were beginning to change and in 1538 a decree was issued stating that every church should make as large a Bible as possible (hence the name of the Bible, the Great Bible) available so that everyone could consult it. The person in charge of this was Miles Coverdale whose version of the Bible used a vast amount of Tyndale's original translation. Unfortunately, the Bible in English was greeted with such enthusiasm (and sung about in ale houses!) that the church authorities feared rebellion and in 1546 many of the English Bibles were burned and ownership was restricted to aristocrats.

During the reign of Queen Mary, who was Roman Catholic and sought to reinstitute Roman Catholicism across England, many Protestant scholars fled. Many of them settled in Geneva and from there published the Geneva Bible in 1560. Two other influential translations before that of the King James Bible were those of the Bishops' Bible in 1568, which though commissioned by Queen Elizabeth does not seem to have been acknowledged by her, and the Douay–Rheims Bible, which was the work of English Roman Catholic scholars who wanted to produce an English language Bible to rival that of the Protestant versions (the New Testament translation was first published in 1582 and the Old Testament in two volumes in 1609 and 1610 respectively).

The King James Version

In 1604, King James I commissioned a new authorized translation of the Bible in response to the concerns of various Puritans who felt that the two previous 'authorized versions' (the Great Bible and the Bishops' Bible) were too Catholic. While the King's original letter said that fifty-four scholars should work on the translation, subsequent lists of translators name only forty-seven people. However many there were at work on the translation, they were split into six companies with two each working in Cambridge, Oxford and Westminster. They split the Bible between them sequentially with:

- the first Westminster company translating Genesis to 2 Kings;
- the first Cambridge company translating 1 Chronicles to the Song of Solomon (also called the Song of Songs);
- the first Oxford company translating the Prophets (Isaiah to Malachi);
- the second Oxford company translating the Gospels, Acts and Revelation;
- the second Westminster company translating the Epistles;
- the second Cambridge company translating the Apocrypha.

Although they translated the New Testament from Greek, the Old Testament from Hebrew and the Apocrypha from a mixture of both Greek and Hebrew, the aim was to produce only very minimal revisions of the Bishops' Bible with supplements from previous translations. However, it is worth noting that, despite this, Tyndale's Bible probably had more influence on the KJV than any other translation with some estimating that over seventy per cent of the KJV is taken from Tyndale.

There are certain stylistic features worthy of note. Unlike in Tyndale's Bible, the translators used Church terms wherever possible (e.g. baptism, church, bishop etc.) to reflect concerns and structures of the Church of England in their day. It may come as more of a surprise to learn that the KJV also deliberately used words that were archaic even when it was translated. So for example, the use of –eth at the end of a third person singular verb (e.g. 'that was the true Light, which lighteth every man that cometh into the world') was widely used in the KJV even though it was not so widely used as it used to be. Equally they used 'thou'/'thee' for the singular 'you', even though 'you' in the singular was widely used at the time.

One of the reasons for the conscious use of archaisms was probably to ensure that the Bible could be understood by the maximum number of people possible. The seventeenth century was a time in which the English language was changing rapidly; the decision to use archaic words meant that the Bible could be used across the whole country where change was taking place at different rates. Another important feature in terms of comprehensibility is the number of words used. The vocabulary of the King James Bible is kept quite limited (at around 8000 words), whereas Shakespeare (whose last play *The Tempest* was probably written in the year that the KJV was published) by comparison is thought to have used upwards of 16,000 words. Again this is to enable the maximum number of people to use and understand the KJV.

In terms of style, probably the most important feature of the KJV – and the feature that ensures its continued popularity today – is that it was translated in order to be read out loud in public. As a result, close attention was paid to the rhetoric and rhythm of the language so that the translations sounded as pleasing to the ear as possible. The translators sat around with the different previous translations before them, as well as the Greek or Hebrew of the text, and tried out phrases orally until they found the one that both communicated what the original language said and sounded best when read out loud. This is one thing that none of the modern translations of the Bible even attempt to do and as a result means that many, particularly those who love poetry and the spoken word, find themselves unsatisfied by even the most accurate of modern translations.

When the KJV was first published it had no name but over time it was given a number of names. In 1797 it was first called the King James' Bible, then the Authorized Version in 1814, the same time as the first use of the phrase 'the King James Version'. Later in the nineteenth century it was called the King James Bible (without the apostrophe). Despite its popularity, the name 'the Authorized Version' is inaccurate for the KJV because there is no evidence that it ever was actually authorized officially. Its worth was heavily disputed for much of the seventeenth century but by the start of the eighteenth century, the KJV was unchallenged as the version used in English Protestant Churches. In fact it became 'so influential that between 1749 and 1752 Bishop Richard Challoner, an English Roman Catholic bishop, produced a new edition of the Douay–Rheims translation (the Roman Catholic English translation originally published in 1610) which shows heavy influence by the KJV.

The need for new translations

What is the best original text?

Once the KJV was established, other translations of the Bible into English became much fewer and far between. The most important translation that took place between the translation of the KJV and the next significant wave of translation was Young's Literal Translation in 1862. Young believed that the Bible needed to be translated exactly as it stood in Hebrew and Greek so that people could see what the text really said. The result is a translation that is, as it sought to be, very close to the original text but often difficult to understand. The first three verses of Genesis illustrate this well: 'In the beginning of God's preparing the heavens and the earth – the earth hath existed waste and void, and darkness *is* on the face of the deep, and the Spirit of God fluttering on the face of the waters, and God saith, "Let light be;" and light is.' Young's translation is a good testament to why absolute literal translation is not always what people need (or want). It is not enough to translate Hebrew words into English words; we also need English sentence structure and idiom in order for the passage to make sense.

Like the KJV, Young's literal translation relied on the Textus Receptus, the edited version of Erasmus' Greek text. The next big revolution in Bible translation concerned the Greek text itself.

One of the great challenges in this area is trying to find out what the Greek (or Hebrew) text of the Bible might have originally looked like. The problem is that when texts are copied by a scribe (which was the only method of reproduction in the ancient world) mistakes are made, normally by accident but sometimes on purpose. Most of the manuscripts of the Bible date to a relatively late period; many later even than the tenth century AD. Textual critics attempt to solve this problem by seeking to weigh the different versions against each other and to work out which might represent the earliest form of the text.

In 1853 two scholars, Westcott and Hort, undertook a revision of the text of the Greek New Testament, which was eventually published in 1881. As a result of their research Westcott and Hort argued that there were four families of New Testament manuscripts: the Byzantine text-type, the Western text-type, the Alexandrian text-type, and the *Codex Sinaiticus* (the latter two had been discovered since Erasmus' edition of the text in the sixteenth century). Each of the families of texts came from a similar origin and bear striking similarities to each other. Erasmus' edition of the text was based on the Byzantine text-type, whereas Westcott and Hort's work was based much more on the Alexandrian text-type and on the *Codex Sinaiticus*. This edition changed the face of translations of the Bible and now, even nearly 150 years on, their decisions and critical principles underlie the modern versions of the Greek text of the New Testament.

The text of the Old Testament has also seen important changes. One of the most important considerations here is the discovery of the Dead Sea Scrolls. As we observed above, they reveal much about a group of Jews who moved out to the desert to pursue their worship of God; equally important, however, is the discovery of manuscripts of the Bible. Indeed about forty per cent of the scrolls found in the caves were biblical manuscripts. The most exciting of these is the Isaiah scroll which is the most complete of all the manuscripts discovered and dated to about 150–100 BC, which makes it in the region of 1100 years older than the Leningrad Codex, the oldest complete manuscript of the Hebrew Bible.

The abandonment of the Textus Receptus

The revolutionary work of Westcott and Hort saw the rise of a new wave of biblical translation, based now on different Greek manuscripts. The first of these was the Revised Version in 1881–5 which, as its name suggests, was a revision of the KJV using the Westcott and Hort Greek manuscripts for the New Testament and, in fact, with Westcott and Hort as two of its over fifty translators. The Revised Version, in its turn, was adapted in the USA as the American Standard Version (ASV) in 1901. The Revised Version marks the beginning of a trend towards more literal translations of the text, at the expense of the poetry and rhetoric of the KJV. In fact, the search for a reliably accurate translation has been one of the reasons for the burgeoning of many, many different translations of the Bible from the period of the Revised Version to the present day.

There are, today, far too many translations available to be able to mention them all but the most influential translations illustrate the different trends in current biblical translation. The next key translation to be published was the Revised Standard Version (RSV) in 1952, which itself was a revision of the American Standard Version of 1901 (in fact its name indicates its heritage – half of it came from the Revised Version and half from the American Standard Version). The panel of translators used the most up-to-date textual editions, including the newly discovered Isaiah scroll from the Dead Sea. The emphasis in the RSV was on the use of the best scholarship available and on bringing the language used up to date (so for example, they moved from using 'thou' and 'thee' to 'you' for human beings, though keeping the 'thou' form for God).

Nevertheless the RSV provoked considerable controversy, particularly in the USA, on the grounds that, for some, it was regarded as far too liberal a translation. In particular, the RSV was criticized for not being literal enough. The translators often decided in favour of the communication of the meaning of the text over the absolutely literal rendering of the Greek or Hebrew. So for example in 1 Corinthians 10.1 where the ASV has 'I would not ... have you ignorant' the RSV has 'I want you to know' and in verse 3 where the ASV says that they 'did all eat the same spiritual food', the RSV has 'and all ate the same supernatural food'. In both cases the ASV is much closer to the Greek than the RSV. Another decision made by the translators of the RSV is a lack of consistency, so that they translated the same Greek or Hebrew words differently depending upon the context in which they were used. One of the most controversial decisions made by the translators of the RSV was to translate Isaiah 7.14 as 'Behold, a young woman shall conceive and bear a son, and shall call his name Immanuel' in contrast to the ASV (and other previous translations) which had 'Behold, the virgin shall conceive and bear a son, and shall call his name Immanuel'. The RSV translators argued that the word used here was more often used to mean young woman than virgin; but because this verse is so closely associated with Matthew's narratives about Jesus' birth in Matthew 1.23 the translators were accused of trying to undermine belief in the virgin birth of Jesus.

Revisions of the revised versions

The controversy about the translational decisions made by the RSV translators did not prevent the RSV from becoming a widely used and very popular translation but it did reignite the King James Only movement, which, as its name suggests, argues for the superiority of the KJV over all other translations (and is slightly bizarrely known as King James Onlyism). The motivations behind those who argue for the King James only vary from those who simply like it better, to those who believe, against most modern scholars, that the Textus Receptus is a better Greek text than the more modern editions and even to those who believe that the KJV itself as a translation was divinely inspired. The controversy also saw the attempt to correct the perceived inaccuracies of the RSV with translations that avoided these issues.

It is possible to trace three major reactions to the RSV which gave rise to three different translations:

- The New King James Version (NJKV) published in 1982 updated the vocabulary and grammar of the KJV while attempting to preserve its style and, due to beliefs about the superiority of the Textus Receptus, used that rather than modern editions of the Greek text of the New Testament.
- The New American Standard Version (NASV) first published in 1971 is a revision of the 1901 ASV and is widely regarded as the most literal translation produced in the twentieth century and is based on a word for word translation of the text. As a result it is also not very easy to read.
- The New International Version (NIV) first published in 1978 is explicitly Protestant (it has not ever translated the Apocrypha) and evangelical and seeks to produce as accurate a translation as possible while at the same time attempting to communicate the meaning of the text. The NIV is very widely popular and well used. It was updated in 2002 as Today's New International Version but this was never very popular, and from 2011 some, though not all, of the changes in the TNIV have been incorporated into the NIV and sold only as that.

Gender-inclusive language

One of the major changes to the NIV made in the TNIV is the use of gender-inclusive language for human beings. So, for example in Romans 8.19 it reads 'creation waits in eager expectation for the children of God to be revealed' as opposed to the NIV which reads 'The creation waits in eager expectation for the sons of God to be revealed'. The TNIV wasn't the first translation to attempt gender-inclusive language; before the TNIV the New Revised Standard Version (NRSV) had made that step in 1989 and the avoidance of masculine-oriented language was one of the major principles that lay behind this particular revision of the RSV. The NRSV was a friendly revision of the RSV seeking to update its language, to make it more relevant for a twenty-first-century readership and to use the best of modern scholarship available as a basis for the translation (particularly the manuscripts of the Dead Sea Scrolls which were by the 1980s more widely available than in 1952).

Although the revisions in the NRSV were wide-ranging, the NRSV is best known for being the first gender-inclusive language version and it is loved or hated – depending on people's views on this subject – accordingly. It is probably worth noting that some of the decisions about gender-inclusive language do change the meaning of verses, sometimes for the better and sometimes for the worse. A significant example of a good change is 2 Corinthians 5.17, which in the RSV translates as 'therefore, if anyone is in Christ, he is a new creation' or the NASV as 'therefore if any man is in Christ, he is a new creature'; in the NRSV this has become 'So if anyone is in Christ, there is a new creation'. As a result Paul is not just talking about an individual change of identity for those in Christ but a much more wide-reaching change for the whole of creation. Pauline scholars often argue that this is what Paul had in mind in this chapter and, as a result, welcome a translation that reflects this.

A much less popular change is made in the Old Testament to a phrase which is then picked up in the New Testament. In the gospels, the phrase 'the Son of Man' is regarded by many as being a crucially important one for understanding who Jesus was.

While in the New Testament the 'Son of Man' is preserved as a phrase in the NRSV, where it occurs in the Old Testament it is often translated as 'one like a human being' (Daniel 7.13). The problem with this is that unless you know that Daniel 7.13 stands behind some of the key uses of Son of Man in the New Testament, the NRSV would not tell you.

The debate rages on about gender-inclusive translations of the Bible. For some it is a normal, natural, even expected method of translation; for others it spoils the text entirely. For some gender-inclusive language reflects more accurately what the author intended to say, for example if the Apostle Paul meant 'brothers and sisters' when he said just 'brothers' why not include this in the translation? Whereas for others the fact that 'brothers and sisters' is not in the original text but 'brothers' is, is a sign that the text should be left alone and read just 'brothers'.

One of the most recent versions of the Bible, the English Standard Version (ESV), regarded the NRSV and the TNIV as departing so far from the original text of the Greek that they began again with another revision of the RSV, called the ESV. Gender-inclusive language was not the only issue at stake for these translators – they were also particularly concerned about the way in which some Old Testament prophecies (often called Messianic prophecies) were translated in such as way that, in the view of the translators of the ESV, they no longer indicated a sufficient expectation of the birth of Jesus.

How literal should the translation be?

The question of gender-inclusive translations throws up probably the most important question of all about Bible translation and this is the question of what makes for the best translation. The assumption that lies behind the NASV is that it is literal, word-for-word translation which is the best translation. So, what this means is that the closer the English is to the original language the better a translation it is. The problem with this is that the NASV is very difficult to read since the translators have put the *words* into English but not the grammar or syntax, and avoid, wherever possible, English idiom. This may seem to be an odd point to make but a particular illustration might make it clearer.

In the famous story of the Wedding at Cana in John 2.1–11, Jesus had a conversation with his mother which is very difficult to put into English. The Greek says literally 'what to me and to you, woman?' (John 2.4). The different English translations on the market make different decisions about how to translate this. Only the Young's Literal translation keeps with what the Greek actually says ('What to me and to thee, woman?') and it is easy to see why. Leaving it as this, means that we the readers are none the wiser as to what Jesus meant when he addressed his mother. As a result, each of the translations has attempted to make sense of what Jesus was saying by working out what they think he was saying. Below is a selection of possible translations:

- And Jesus said to her, 'Woman, what have I to do with you?' (NASV)
- And Jesus said to her, 'Woman, what does this have to do with me?' (ESV)
- 'Woman, why do you involve me?' Jesus replied. (NIV)
- Jesus said, 'Woman, what do you want from me?' (New Jerusalem Bible)
- Jesus said to her, 'Woman, what does your concern have to do with Me?' (NKJV)
- 'How does that concern you and me?' Jesus asked. (New Living Translation)
- And Jesus said to her, 'Woman, what concern is that to you and to me?' (NRSV)

Two things are clear from this. Firstly no one can agree about what Jesus meant and secondly if we want to understand what is going on, then even the most literal translations have to interpret the words in order to make sense of them.

This brings us to the field of translation theory, and the question of what makes for the best translation. Translation theory raises the question of the principles that lie behind the decisions translators make as they choose how to put a text in one language into another language. Translation theory has a spectrum of methods with, at one end, something called formal equivalence and at the other end dynamic or functional equivalence. Formal equivalence is what you might call ultra-literal or word-for-word translation. Here you take each word of a text and try and find another word in English to translate it with. The most extreme formal equivalence does not try too hard to fit the translation into English grammar and syntax and instead just translates each word as it comes. As we saw with the translations from John 2.4, this means that you end up with quite an accurate transfer of a text from one language to another but once you have finished it doesn't necessarily communicate very much. Anyone who has used an online translation programme will understand the pitfalls of extreme formal equivalence, in that you end up with a string of words in English that do not mean anything.

At the other end of the spectrum lies dynamic or functional equivalence. Dynamic equivalence does not attempt to do a word-for-word translation but weighs phrases at a time and tries to communicate the meaning that lies behind the text. Extreme dynamic equivalence seeks to be idiomatic and to use phrases, or even colloquialisms, to get the best meaning across. Connected to dynamic equivalence are paraphrases, which would be even further along the spectrum at the opposite end of formal equivalence, were it not for the fact that paraphrases are not translations. Paraphrases take already existing English translations and put them into modern language and idiom.

It will come as no surprise at all that this whole area is hotly contested. In some circles, formal equivalence is the only good method of translation, whereas in others the communication of the meaning of the text is far, far more important than rendering it word for word. An illustration of the differences in translation that the different theories produce can be seen by the two translations below. The first comes from the NASV which is, as has been noted above, one of the most literal (i.e. using formal equivalence) of the modern English translations. The second comes from the Message which is an extremely idiomatic dynamic translation. The verses are Romans 12.1–2 and sound very different in each translation

> I urge you therefore, brethren, by the mercies of God, to present your bodies a living and holy sacrifice, acceptable to God, which is your spiritual service of worship. And do not be conformed to this world, but be transformed by the renewing of your mind, that you may prove what the will of God is, that which is good and acceptable and perfect. (NASV)

> So here's what I want you to do, God helping you: Take your everyday, ordinary life – your sleeping, eating, going-to-work, and walking-around life – and place it before God as an offering. Embracing what God does for you is the best thing you can do for him. Don't become so well-adjusted to your culture that you fit into it without even thinking. Instead, fix your attention on God. You'll be changed from the inside out. Readily recognize what he wants from you, and quickly respond to it. Unlike the culture around you, always dragging you down to its level of immaturity, God brings the best out of you, develops well-formed maturity in you.
>
> (The Message)

These two illustrate the values and challenges of each. The NASV tries to be as close to the Greek as possible and by doing so introduces what are to many twenty-first-century readers alien and bewildering concepts, like sacrifice. The Message puts the meaning into language that many people today can relate to but is so idiomatic that it comes down to personal taste, and for some people the Message is not to their personal taste.

In reality nearly all modern translations are a mixture of both formal and dynamic equivalence. The question is simply how close to each end of the spectrum each aims to be. The NASV aims to be as close as it can to the end of formal equivalence but as we noticed with John 2.4 above even the NASV has to make dynamic equivalence decisions with difficult verses. Also close to the formal equivalence end of the spectrum are the family of 'standard version' translations: the RSV, NRSV and ESV. Interestingly the NIV deliberately attempted to be a midpoint between formal and dynamic equivalence and aims for as much accuracy as possible while communicating the essence of the message.

Other translations that we haven't talked about yet are more towards the dynamic equivalence end of translation. These include the New English Bible (1970, revised in 1989 as the Revised English Bible), the Good News Bible (1976), the Contemporary English Version (1995), the New Living Translation (1996) and the Message (2002). Almost by definition because they are idiomatic there are many more of them than of the other translations and they need constant updates as the idiom changes. Dynamic equivalence translations are often looked down on by those who favour formal equivalence as being overly interpretative, though in reality all translations are interpretations of the text since the choice of words and phrases used interpret what the text is really saying. It is just that the interpretation is more obvious in some translations than in others.

There are no very recent paraphrases of the Bible. Those which are often called paraphrases, like the Message, are in fact not paraphrases at all in that their translators worked from the original text, not from an English translation. These modern translations are genuine translations but they are simply highly idiomatic. There were, however, two hugely influential para-phrases. The first was by someone called J.B. Phillips who was a Church of England minister in the 1950s. He became con-cerned that the young people in his church could not relate to the Bible. So he paraphrased it into language that they would be able to understand and published it bit by bit, until in 1958 it came out as *The New Testament in Modern English*. *The Living Bible* was another attempt at this and was produced by Kenneth N. Taylor in 1971. Although initially very popular and widely adopted, hesitations about paraphrases became so great that when *The Living Bible* was revised in the 1980s, and published as *The New Living Translation* in 1996, it was in fact no longer a paraphrase but now a translation from the original text.

Both of these paraphrases had a profound impact on modern biblical translation. Although paraphrases are largely abandoned today, they illustrated the kind of fresh dynamic approach that can make the Bible come alive for a modern audience. This kind of approach is now found in translations that lean more towards dynamic equivalence but the influence of J.B. Phillips and *The Living Bible* lives on. People often ask why there needs to be so many different translations. Indeed the task of going into a book-shop and buying a Bible gets more and more difficult as time goes on and the choice gets wider and wider. The answer to the question of why there needs to be so many is idiom. As soon as idiom becomes important then personal taste comes to the fore. What I might like may not be the same as what you might like. Do you like or loathe colloquial language? Does American phraseology help you to understand things or simply annoy you? Do you like a Bible that uses modern terms or are you more comfortable with archaisms? All of these factors come into play when people choose a Bible to read, and as a result there is a vast array of possible choices.

Roman Catholic translations of Scripture

So far in this chapter we have looked primarily at Protestant translations of Scripture, not least because the Protestant desire to produce Bibles in people's own languages is what has led to the proliferation of translations available. It is important, however, to recognize that there are also Roman Catholic translations of Scripture which are equally important. This tradition goes back to the Douay–Rheims Bible which, as we saw above, was first published in the late sixteenth–early seventeenth century, and later revised by Bishop Challoner between 1749 and 1752. The Douay–Rheims version was authorized by the Roman Catholic Church and used in public worship well into the twentieth century.

In 1943 Pope Pius XII encouraged Roman Catholics to translate the Bible from the original languages. This gave rise to three key translations:

- The Jerusalem Bible (1966) is widely admired as a translation that is both literal and literary (i.e. it is close to the text but in fluent and attractive English). The Jerusalem Bible was translated from the original languages but also used a modern French translation *La Bible de Jérusalem* for inspiration. The Jerusalem Bible was revised and published in 1985 as the New Jerusalem Bible. Opinion is split over whether it is better or worse than the Jerusalem Bible.
- In the same year as the publication of the Jerusalem Bible, the RSV Catholic edition (RSV-CE) was published. This was not a Roman Catholic translation but an adaptation of the Protestant RSV. As a result the deuterocanonical literature can be found in the text itself, rather than separated from the rest of the Old Testament, and certain key phrases, important to Roman Catholic doctrine, are revised. The most important

of these is Gabriel's greeting to Mary which is 'Hail, full of grace' not 'Hail, O favored one' as in the RSV. The Roman Catholic Church did not approve of the changes in the NRSV and so have never adopted it. Instead they re-issued the RSV-CE with the archaic forms removed in 2006.

- The New American Bible (1970) is a translation by American Roman Catholics and is used in the USA but not generally in Britain. It was revised in 1986.

All of the Roman Catholic translations, as you would expect, contain the deuterocanonical literature scattered throughout the Old Testament as it is in the Septuagint, and not bound separately – or omitted entirely – as in Protestant Bibles.

Jewish translations of the Tanakh

Another family of translations that we should not overlook are Jewish translations. The first of these to be published by a committee was the Jewish Publication Society of America Version in 1917. It is, of course, based on the Masoretic text of the Hebrew Bible but used both the Revised Version's and the American Standard Version's Old Testament for ideas. Again, as you would expect, the order of the books are as in the Masoretic text and ordered according to Torah, Prophets and Writings.

This translation was replaced in 1985 by the New Jewish Publication Society translation (NJPS), which was an entirely fresh translation of the Bible and not dependent on any other previously published translation. It was produced by a team of high quality scholars who have produced a stimulating and accurate translation of the Masoretic text. There is also a 'gender-sensitive' version of this translation called the Contemporary Torah.

Non-English translations of the Bible

The vast majority of this chapter has dealt with English translations of the Bible, not least because this book is written in English, but it would be wrong to leave a chapter about translation without an acknowledgement of the extent and significance of the Bible around the world. It is thought that the Bible in full has been translated into around 450 languages, though parts of the Bible are available in nearly 2500 languages.

This translation work is undertaken both by individuals and by organizations. The United Bible Societies are the biggest of these, and is an association of over 145 member societies which work in more than 200 countries worldwide. Many Bible societies are ecumenical and non-denominational. In contrast the other big Bible translation organization, the Wycliffe Bible Translators, was founded to be solely Protestant and remains so. The work of these two continues to be hugely important as they seek to translate the Bible into the languages of those who want to read it.

Probably the most common question that I am asked is 'which is the best Bible translation?' The answer, as I hope has become clear throughout this chapter, is that it all depends upon what you want. Factors to bear in mind are:

- how close to the original language you want the translation to be;
- how idiomatic you would like the translation to be;
- whether you want the translation to include archaisms or modern language;
- whether you want a Protestant, Roman Catholic or Jewish translation;
- whether you want the translation to be gender-inclusive or not;
- whether you want a translation that stands in a line of translations or one that is fresher and less influenced by previous decisions;

- whether you want the translation to be based on the Textus Receptus or on more modern critical editions of the text.

The list could go on and on. The point is that most modern translations are good, but each has its stronger points and its weaker points. The best advice, in my view, is to have access to more than one translation and to choose those that represent different translational decisions both in terms of formal versus dynamic equivalence and in terms of denomination and religion but most of all to choose a translation that you like and are most likely to read.

5

Interpretation

One of the main objections to biblical interpretation is that so often biblical interpretation just seems to make the Bible more complicated. 'Why', people ask, 'can't you just take it at face value and leave it at that? Why do you have to make it so hard?' The answer is because every time we read anything we interpret it.

Imagine receiving a letter through the post. We can, often without realizing it, interpret a vast amount simply by looking at the envelope. We work out where it is from, from the postmark and stamp, when it was posted again from the postmark, we work out if is more likely to be a personal or business letter from whether the address is handwritten or typed and from what type of envelope it is. Then, depending on who we are and what is going on in our lives, we make decisions about which letters to open first. I normally always open personal letters first, unless I know I am expecting an important business letter when I might open that first instead. This somewhat complex interpretation of the letters we receive day by day is something we normally do without even batting an eyelid (often in fact without even realizing we've done it).

As a result, whether people know they are doing it or not, anyone who reads the Bible is already interpreting it. Biblical interpretation encourages consciously slowing down the process of interpretation so that the different steps can be reflected on in more detail. We need to do this because, although the Bible offers us clues similar to the ones that letters give us when they arrive, because it was written so long ago they are clues that we only occasionally pick up. The process of biblical interpretation is often very similar to what we do with envelopes. We look for clues about where the books were written, when, and by whom. We also look for clues about what style was used in writing the books and finally we recognize that who we are and what we think can make a difference to the way in which we read texts.

These three categories of issues are often called by modern scholars behind the text (i.e. the exploration of the history of the text), on or in the text (i.e. the exploration of the literary nature of the text), and in front of the text questions (i.e. the exploration of the issues that the readers bring to the text). The second half of this chapter will be focused on these three questions and on asking how they help us to understand the Bible better, but before we go there it is worth taking a quick glance at some of the ways in which the Bible has been interpreted through the centuries.

The interpretation of the Bible through the centuries

Interpretation of the Bible in the Bible

The place to begin is with the recognition that the Bible has always been interpreted and re-interpreted. The question is never whether it is interpreted – but how. Even the Old Testament interpreted other parts of the Old Testament. So for example, 2 Chronicles 36.20–1:

> He took into exile in Babylon those who had escaped from the sword, and they became servants to him and to his sons until the establishment of the kingdom of Persia, to fulfil the word of the LORD by the mouth of Jeremiah, until the land had made up for its Sabbaths. All the days that it lay desolate it kept Sabbath, to fulfil seventy years.

quotes Jeremiah 25.11 ('This whole land shall become a ruin and a waste, and these nations shall serve the king of Babylon seventy years,' Jeremiah 25.11) but it also explains it. 2 Chronicles clarifies why it is that the people needed to be away from the land for seventy years. The reason is so that the land can lie fallow and recover from the sins of the people.

Intriguingly enough Daniel 9 picks this up and reinterprets it again throughout the whole chapter. Many modern scholars would accept that the book of Daniel was written in the second century BC (i.e. over 350 years after the end of the exile). Daniel 9 appears to be explaining why the people are still emotionally in exile over 350 years since they were meant to have returned. God's answer to Daniel indicates that the 'seventy years' have now become symbolic and are the symbolic time before an anointed prince will come to save his people.

This method of interpretation which takes a biblical prophecy and shows how it relates to a community from a different time isn't just found in the Bible itself but was popular in Second Temple Judaism as well. In particular, the authors of the Dead Sea Scrolls show an especial liking for this form of interpretation. They liked to take the visions and prophecies of the Bible and demonstrate how they related to their own situation. One of the most famous of these is the Commentary (or Pesher) on Habakkuk. This text comes from the Dead Sea Scrolls of Qumran and is thought to date to the late first century BC. It interprets the enemies faced by Habakkuk's original audience as the Romans who were perceived to be threatening the Qumran community. The reason why they did this was because they believed that they were living in a time when the prophecies and visions were beginning to come true. As a result they described their experiences in terms of the fulfilment of long expected prophecies from the Bible.

This is also true, if not more so, of the New Testament writers who believed that the coming of Jesus marked the fulfilment of all previous prophecies. As a result the New Testament writers set

out to demonstrate as far as they could that Jesus was this fulfilment. They did this in all sorts of ways:

- By quoting directly from the Bible and showing how Jesus
  fulfilled it. See for example Matthew 1.22–23 ('All this took
  place to fulfil what had been spoken by the Lord through the
  prophet: "Look, the virgin shall conceive and bear a son, and
  they shall name him Emmanuel," which means, "God is with
  us."'). This is a quotation from Isaiah 7.14 which promised to
  Ahaz a sign that God would protect him from a current threat
  in the form of the birth of a baby. Matthew took this prophecy and interpreted Jesus' birth as its fulfilment.
- Another way in which this happened was typology, a technique
  that connects similar types of events or ideas together. An
  example of this can be found in John's Gospel when Moses' lift-
  ing up of the snake in the wilderness (Numbers 21.8) is likened
  to Jesus' death on the cross (John 3.14). Here one event is read
  in the light of the other event and seen to be a fulfilment of it.
- The New Testament writers also liked to join Old Testament
  passages together and use them together to show that Jesus
  fulfils the prophecy; for example 1 Peter 2.4–8 links together
  Isaiah 28.16 and Psalm 118.22 and uses them as a proof of
  Jesus' fulfilment of the prophecies about stones.

The list of how the New Testament writers used the Old
Testament could go on and on but the few examples given here
illustrate well the way in which the New Testament writers used
the Old Testament to understand the world in which they lived.

Interpretation of the Bible in the early and medieval periods

In chapter 3 we traced the slow journey of the books that
eventually became a part of the New Testament towards being

accepted as authoritative. As these books became more widely accepted and acknowledged, the question of how they should be interpreted began to emerge. In the earliest period the writers who are often called the Apostolic Fathers, a label that refers to those writing until the end of the second century AD, continued to focus on the way in which Jesus fulfilled the prophecies of the Old Testament, as the New Testament writers had. A particularly famous example of this was Irenaeus, bishop in Lugdunum in Gaul until 202 AD who spent a whole chapter of one of his books, called *Against Heresies*, demonstrating why Jesus was the fulfilment of Isaiah 7.14.

By the end of the second century, however, disagreements were already beginning to emerge about how the Bible should be interpreted. Two distinct schools of thought grew up: one based in Alexandria in Egypt and the other in Antioch in Syria.

The Alexandrian school focused on allegorical readings of the text. What this means is that they saw the Bible as having at least two layers of meaning: the literal meaning and a symbolic meaning. This view sees the Bible as a complex web of symbols which, if read correctly, can point to deep truths. The key was to work out what was being symbolized at any one time. Probably the most famous member of the Alexandrian school was Origen, a scholar and theologian of the third century AD. Origen saw complex allegories in nearly all of Scripture. For example he thought that the sacrifices referred to in the book of Leviticus should be read as the spiritual sacrifice of Christians, or that Joshua's conquering of the Promised Land should be seen as referring to the salvation of Christians. In many ways, this is simply an extension – made possible by the use of Greek philosophy and its interest in ideals – of the method we have already seen of taking the Bible and showing how it relates to another era.

ORIGEN OF ALEXANDRIA

We know most of what we know about Origen from Eusebius who wrote a century or so later.

Origen was born in Alexandria in around 185 BC. His Christian father was martyred in 202 AD in the persecution that took place during the reign of the Roman Emperor Septimius Severus. Eusebius maintains that Origen was only seventeen when he became the teacher at the Christian catechetical school of Alexandria. He was well trained both in the Bible and in Greek philosophy and he is still renowned as a profound commentator on the Bible as well as an astute philosopher. Indeed his work *On First Principles* is still regarded today as a very fine philosophical text.

Origen was an ascetic and believed strongly in abstaining from 'worldly pleasures'. As a result, eventually he sold his library and lived frugally off the proceeds. Eusebius also recounts that he took Matthew 19.12 (which is a saying of Jesus about eunuchs) so literally that he castrated himself so that he could teach women as well as men without raising any suspicions.

Origen had a number of conflicts with his bishop Demetrius which culminated in Demetrius banishing him from Alexandria when Origen was ordained outside of Egypt in Caesarea. In 231 Origen moved to Caesarea and became renowned for his battle against Christianity's opponents, and was often sent to correct heresies.

Origen died around 254 as a result of the torture he received during another persecution of Christians, this time under the Emperor Decius.

Many years after his death in the fifth century, Origen was posthumously denounced by the synod of Constantinople in 543 and some of his teaching declared heretical a century later by the fifth ecumenical council in 553. The question of his orthodoxy still causes much debate among scholars, though there can be no doubt that he was a very fine thinker and writer.

The Alexandrian school came into considerable conflict with the Antiochene school who, although they did not deny the validity of an allegorical approach to Scripture, opposed the particular way in which the Alexandrian school did it. The Antiochene school preferred to seek the plain meaning of the text rather than the complex, sometimes fanciful deep meanings sought by the Alexandrians. The importance of the allegorical reading of Scripture was cemented a century or so later by Augustine, bishop of Hippo in the late fourth and early fifth centuries, who argued strongly for both a literal and an allegorical meaning of the text. In particular, he believed that the whole of the Old Testament could, if you tried hard enough, be seen as prophesying the coming of Jesus Christ.

These ways of reading the Bible laid foundations for the way in which the Bible was read in the Middle Ages. By then, influenced by another bishop of the early Church – Gregory the Great who was pope from 590–604 AD – there were believed to be four major ways of interpreting the Bible:

- literal, i.e. the plain meaning of the text;
- allegorical, i.e. the symbolic meaning of the text. A medieval example of this comes from St Bede, a monk from Jarrow (c.672–735) who understood Elkanah and his two wives Peninah and Hannah (1 Samuel 1.2) as Christ with the synagogue and the church;
- moral application of the text, i.e. the meaning of the text that helps Christians to live righteously;
- anagogical, i.e. the sense of the text that points towards the eternal. Similar to allegorical interpretation, anagogical interpretation understands the events of the Bible as pointing towards a heavenly existence. So the parting of the Red Sea is seen as pointing towards God bridging the gap between heaven and earth.

Interpretation of the Bible during the Reformation and beyond

One of the major differences between the biblical interpretation of the medieval period and that of the Reformation is that the Reformers sought, wherever possible, to read the text of the Bible in its original language (and of course to translate it into the language that ordinary people spoke too). The period of the Reformation saw a great revival in the study of Scripture and, in particular, an emphasis on the Scriptures themselves rather than interpretations of them. For many years, the Church's interpretation of Scripture – particularly that of the early Church Fathers – was seen as being almost as important as Scripture itself. The Reformers, in contrast, believed firmly in what they called *sola scriptura* (which means 'by Scripture alone'); in other words, they believed only that which could be found in Scripture.

Martin Luther (1483–1546), who is credited by many people as being the father of the Reformation, rejected the medieval four-fold interpretation of Scripture and adopted instead a much more literal approach. Having said this, he, like many Christians before him, looked at the Old Testament primarily as containing prophecies about Jesus Christ and was much less interested in those parts of the Old Testament which clearly have nothing to say about Christ, like the book of Esther. Equally importantly, Luther refused to engage in speculation about things which were not in the Bible. For example, he viewed medieval speculations about angels and demons as being particularly irrelevant and insisted instead on talking about only that which could be known about from the Bible itself.

One of the striking features about the Reformation is that it marked a shift of interest from the gospels to the Pauline epistles. Indeed Luther's interest in Paul's doctrine of justification by faith alone became one of the major lenses through which the writers of the Reformation viewed the interpretation of Scripture.

In the hundred years or so that followed the Reformation, one of the doctrines that became increasingly important was that of the verbal inspiration of Scripture (i.e. the idea that each word it contained came directly from God). This in turn led to the belief in biblical infallibility. If each word came from God then the words themselves must be true and unerring.

Interpretation of the Bible in the modern and postmodern periods

It was the changing circumstances of the world that was the impetus for the next move in biblical interpretation. The period of the Enlightenment saw Western perceptions of the world shift and change. The discovery of new lands and increasingly rapid scientific discovery made it clearer and clearer that the old ways of viewing the world and faith needed to be re-evaluated. One of the key factors in this was the growing emphasis on the importance of reason for humanity and the recognition that faith, as well as everything else in the world, should properly be subjected to reflection and evaluation.

One of the primary ways in which this began to demonstrate itself was in an interest in how, when and where the books of the Bible came to be written. As a result in the eighteenth century there grew up a number of theories about the sources that lie behind the text of the Bible and what they tell us about who might have written and edited them and why. This way of reading the text became known as the historical-critical method and sought primarily to understand how oral tradition passed on the earliest accounts; how these oral narratives slowly began to be written down as texts; and how the 'biblical writers' (who in effect become more like editors than writers) edited these sources so that, eventually, after a process of copying by scribes and translating, we ended up with the books as they lie before us today.

One of the key principles of this type of interpretation was that it treated the Bible not as sacred Scripture but as you would treat any historical book. The values and principles of the eighteenth and nineteenth centuries demanded that 'objectivity' was considered to be more important than anything else for achieving the best, reasoned interpretation of the Bible. As a result the Bible was not regarded as sacred, or even as Scripture, but just another text in a panoply of other texts. The implication of this is that the historical-critical method was much more interested in the origins of texts – in the authors and the dates of and locations of writing – than they were in the theology contained in the text.

As the twentieth century began and developed, however, philosophers, especially those like Martin Heidegger (1889–1976), began to recognize that it was impossible to interpret texts – or indeed anything else – entirely objectively. We all bring presuppositions to what we do and these colour and change how we view it. In addition, scholars also began to recognize that a purely historical approach to the Bible simply did not do justice to what the Bible was trying to say. Since the mid-twentieth century biblical interpretation has become more and more diverse. The study of hermeneutics (the technical term which refers to the science of interpretation) has become increasingly philosophical in its approach and a discipline in its own right.

For much of the twentieth century, the historical-critical method maintained its dominance over the study of the Bible but towards the end of the twentieth century, cracks began to appear in this dominance. For many years, scholars held the belief (at least implicitly) that if they could hone their method sufficiently well then they would be able to produce the perfect, scientific method which could re-create beyond the shadow of a doubt the historical origins of a text. What has happened instead is that scholars have produced more and increasingly diverse ranges of possible origins of the texts which present readers with a bewildering array of possibilities. Confidence that the perfect solution could be found began to waver, at least for some.

The cracks in the edifice of the reliability of the historical-critical method caused some (though by no means all) biblical scholars to explore alternative methods of reading the Bible. This exploration was also influenced by the rise of what many people call postmodernism, which is a loosely connected collection of responses to the rationalism of modernism, characterized particularly by a scepticism about the desire for or indeed achievability of objectivity and by the willingness to juxtapose different ideas and ways of viewing the world.

As these other methods of reading the Bible became more and more popular, different approaches became apparent. Some focused attention on the text itself and asked questions about the language it used or the rhetoric it employed, whereas others began to pay more attention to the readers, either noting or encouraging the subjectivity of the reader involved.

As we make our way through the early twenty-first century, it becomes harder to describe biblical interpretation. The methods that people use to interpret the text become more and more diverse (and often more complex) so that those encountering them for the first time can feel overwhelmed simply by the range of what is on offer. Some scholars maintain the principles of the historical-critical method; others use insights from other disciplines (like the social sciences) to shed light on biblical interpretation; others still focus on particular subjectivities (such as feminism) that people might bring to the text and reflect on how this might change the way the text is read. Most important of all is variety. While some scholars still focus solely on the history behind the text, a good number of people focus on a range of approaches and might be interested in, for example, the rhetoric of the text from a post-colonial perspective, or the history of the text from an ecological perspective.

So how should you interpret the Bible?

Given this ever-increasing complexity in the area of biblical interpretation, it can feel as though the non-specialist has no hope at all of being able to interpret the Bible. Indeed it may well be possible to observe a correlation between the complexity of the methods of biblical interpretation and the growth of what might be called non-critical methods of engaging with the text. In other words, one of the unforeseen outcomes of the increased sophistication of biblical criticism is that it has become such an apparently labyrinthine area that many readers of the Bible simply opt not to enter it at all.

Non-critical engagement with the Bible is far from new; indeed the term non- or pre-critical interpretation is often used to describe all readings of the Bible before the Enlightenment (in other words before the eighteenth century). The Enlightenment, as we have seen, introduced to biblical studies (as well as to many other areas of life) the notion of criticism, in the sense of using your critical faculties to engage with the text rather than just accepting it as it stands. Pre- or non-critical readings of the text are those which do not use these critical faculties to engage with the text. What some of the most popular modern methods of reading the Bible share in common with the pre-critical readings is a concern to apply what the Bible says directly to the life, concerns and experiences of the reader rather than the more detailed exploration of critical issues.

Lectio Divina

One method which has seen a particular resurgence in the past few years is a technique known as *Lectio Divina* (which means literally divine or holy reading). *Lectio Divina* is a classic pre-critical approach to the Bible because it emerged with St Benedict (*c*.480–547) who was the founder of the Benedictine Order. Benedict instructed his monks 'to listen … with the ears of your heart' to Scripture (from the prologue of the *Rule of St Benedict*). This simple command was expanded by later writers and thinkers and was cast by a later writer, the Carthusian monk Guigo II (d. 1193), into a four-fold pattern of prayer: reading, meditation, prayer and contemplation. The idea of *Lectio Divina* is that a passage is read out loud and the hearers listen carefully for a word that lights up for them. The hearer then meditates on that word, allowing it to interact with who they are. After this they bring what they have learnt to God in prayer, and finally sit in stillness to rest in the presence of God. In this encounter with the text there is little need or desire for critical engagement. This kind of non-critical encounter with the text raises the question of whether anything other than a simple listening to the text is necessary for those who wish to read the Bible today.

The key question in response to this is who is listening to the text, where, and why. *Lectio Divina* can be a powerful tool for engaging with the Bible in a context of faith where the primary goal is devotion and encounter with God, but not everyone who reads the Bible does so from a position of faith, and even those who do read it from a position of faith do so in a variety of contexts and for a variety of reasons. Reading the Bible is not a 'one size fits all' experience and consequently requires more than one method of engagement.

Lectio Divina is valuable in some contexts but not in others and it achieves some things but not others. For example, *Lectio Divina* cannot give the reader a sense of anything but the detailed words of that particular passage. It cannot introduce the reader to the way in which different passages in a particular book relate to each other, nor to how a story or rhetoric message builds up through a book to press a message home. It cannot illustrate how the texts of the Old Testament interpret other parts of the Old Testament nor how the New Testament uses Old Testament texts.

Lectio Divina is a method of reading the Bible which focuses on detail but a good knowledge of the Bible also requires a bigger picture which explores more of whole books or even of the whole canon of Scripture.

This method of reading the Bible is one of a range of ways of reading the Bible that fall under the heading 'devotional reading'. There are many more and all of them focus primarily around what the Bible has to say about the lives of those who are reading it today. Academic readings of the Bible, obviously, do not have this as their major focus. Their major focus varies depending on the method used, from getting to know the historical context of the text to offering challenging readings based on presuppositions brought to the text. This does not mean that these methods cannot be used by those who wish to read the text devotionally; of course they can, but their primary goal is not devotional – it is getting to know the text as well as possible.

Behind, on and in front of the text readings of the Bible

Nevertheless these more academic readings offer something important to all those who seek to interpret the Bible for themselves since they raise at least some of the questions that need to be asked in order to achieve a good all-round understanding of the Bible. These are the questions we raised at the start of this chapter, which can be organized under the general headings of:

- behind the text (i.e. questions about the events recorded in the text and how the text came to be written down);
- on or in the text (i.e. questions about the text itself, its shape, language and style);
- in front of the text (i.e. questions about the reader who is reading the text, in particular what presuppositions they bring to their reading of the text).

Even if you do not want to engage in the level of technical detail that some academic readings of the text demand, these three are valuable questions to ask in order to ensure that the Bible has been explored in as much breadth and depth as possible.

Behind the text

Behind the text readings of the Bible focus, as the name suggests, on what happened before the text reached its final form. These readings that focus on what happens behind the text trace a long, and sometimes complex, journey from the original event to the Bible that we now have before us. Many of the concerns of the historical–critical movement can be identified as behind the text readings.

We begin with the event itself. The easiest example to use to illustrate the whole of this process is the gospels and their stories about Jesus, but this can work for many different parts of the Bible too. In this instance the original event was Jesus walking and talking in Galilee and then Jerusalem. These original events were talked about by the earliest Christians. The stories were told and the details discussed. This is what is called the oral tradition where the stories were passed from person to person as they remembered and talked about what they had seen and heard.

From here these stories slowly began to be written down in written sources. Precisely when this happened is not entirely clear. The evidence of Papias, the second-century bishop of Hierapolis, is that well into the second century, Christians, like Papias, preferred eyewitness oral accounts over written texts but since most scholars believe that all the gospels had been completed by this point it is clear that this does not mean that there were no written sources before the second century. What is most likely is that the oral tradition and written sources overlapped for quite some time until the eyewitness accounts (even those handed down a generation or so) had died out and were replaced entirely by written accounts. The written sources, however, were probably not the gospels themselves but collections of stories and sayings which were, in their turn, used by the gospel writers to shape and craft the gospel they wrote. Many New Testament scholars believe that the gospel writers specifically shaped their gospel in order to respond to the particular concerns of their own community and to answer the questions that they raised.

There is a particular form of biblical criticism associated with each of these stages as the table below illustrates.

Stage	The name of the criticism	What it involves
The original event	Historical or social scientific criticism	An exploration of the culture, history and society from the time when the event took place in order to shed more light on what the Bible says.
Oral tradition	Form criticism	An exploration of the form in which the oral tradition relayed the story and an attempt to work out how it might have changed as the story was told and retold.
The first written sources	Source criticism	The attempt to find evidence behind the text to indicate which written sources were used by the gospel writers to construct their gospel.
The final gospels	Redaction criticism	The attempt to see the ways in which the gospel writers used the sources before them and shaped them for their own audience.

The majority of people reading the Bible will not notice evidence of oral tradition or of redaction in the text; sometimes, however, the gaps in the text are so clear that they beg the question of how they got there. Take, for example, the end of John 14.31, when Jesus said to the disciples 'Rise, let us be on our way' but then stays talking for another three chapters until eventually they go at the start of John 18. The most common explanation for this is that chapters 15–17 of John are additional written material which has been inserted into the original text because the content seems to fit with the rest (which indeed it does seem to do) and may well indicate something about how this text came to be put together.

Another example can be found in Matthew's Gospel which makes a reference to disciples being handed over to their 'councils and flogged in their synagogues' (Matthew 10.17). There is little evidence that this would have happened at the time of Jesus, but it may have happened later at the time that Matthew was writing his gospel, especially if, as scholars suspect, he was writing his gospel to a community that was in conflict with some of their Jewish neighbours. This reference, and others like it, may be able to shine a light on the community to whom Matthew was writing and on the issues that concerned them when it was written. When reading the Bible, it is worth being alert to geography that doesn't fit, to phrases that seem oddly inserted, and to events that may be anachronistic since all of these could point to evidence about the history of composition of the text.

Much more important than how the text was put together are the insights that can be gleaned simply from knowing historical details about the time when the text was either set or written (or both). Over and over again new light is shed upon well-known texts by knowing some historical details. This could be as simple as knowing when certain texts were set. So for example knowing that the book of Lamentations is set just after the temple has been destroyed in the exile of 586 BC, or that Isaiah 40 and its great message of hope is written to the people of God as they were about to return from exile, helps us to understand much more about the text itself.

Or it could throw up more complex issues such as that the history reported in the book of Daniel doesn't quite fit the history of the Persian period. So for example in Daniel 4, Daniel interprets the dream of Nebuchadnezzar as indicating that the king would go mad. There is little evidence that Nebuchadnezzar was ever mad but there is evidence of the madness of Nabonidus, the last king of Babylon, who went into self-exile in the middle of the desert in Teima during his reign (some of the most interesting evidence for this is a fragment from Qumran known as *The Prayer of Nabonidus*). Another example is that Belshazzar who is called a king in Daniel was only ever a co-regent ruling while his father, Nabonidus, was in exile in Teima. There is other evidence as well but all this points to the author of Daniel knowing the history of the period only vaguely which suggests that it may not have been written at the time of Daniel but at a later date.

So knowledge of the history behind the book can help to give texture and added depth to texts but it can also help us to understand what is going on in the narrative itself. Often the texts of the Bible are written into a period so different from our own that it is almost impossible for us to understand the cultural references or expectations that lie behind the text. Some knowledge of the history can simply cast into clearer light features that might otherwise make little sense. An example of this is the story of the Samaritan woman whom Jesus met at the well in John 4. It is often assumed that because she had had five husbands and that the person she then had as a husband was not married to her indicates that she is 'a sinner'. However, the realization that women at the time of Jesus were not able to divorce their husbands and that some husbands divorced their wives on the flimsiest of excuses (e.g. Rabbi Hillel says that a man might divorce his wife for burning a meal), added to the fact that at no point did Jesus suggest that the woman was in the wrong, all indicates that she was probably more hurt than sinning. This means that the conversation between Jesus and the woman changes from being a conversation about sin into a conversation about healing.

This kind of historical information begins to transform a reading of the text so that it begins to make more sense to people reading it today. Nevertheless, people often ask – with a certain level of frustration, it must be acknowledged – how they are meant to get to know that kind of historical detail. The answer is that it is not necessary to know all of this information already but what is important is to be able to realize when you need to know it and, then, to know where to look to find the answers you need.

Probably the most important skill anyone needs for reading the Bible well is curiosity. Critical readings of the text are primarily readings stimulated by curiosity of all kinds. Indeed the best tool for reading behind the text is the use of the question 'why?' Why did this happen then? Why did the characters say what they did? Why did other characters expect a certain thing to happen? The questions that simple curiosity evokes are the questions that lead to some of the best interpretations of the Bible.

The next most important skill is knowing where to look for answers. The best and most skilled chefs probably don't use recipe books, but the rest of us do. The point about being a good cook is not that you know all the recipes you could ever want already but instead that you know where to go to find the recipes you need. The same is true of Biblical interpretation: a combination of good background books and commentaries should mean that you have all the information you might need at your fingertips for when you do need it.

On or in the text

On or in the text readings of the Bible focus particularly on the text itself. Some of the issues that we have already explored in this book fall into this aspect of Biblical interpretation.

Chapter 2's exploration of the style or genre of each part of the Bible is one method of interpretation that pays particular attention to the text of the Bible. One of the factors that significantly affects how we read the Bible is what we think we are reading in the first place. Consequently the decision about what style of writing we are reading makes a big difference to how we interpret the text. In chapter 2 we explored the general style of each book of the Bible but, of course, styles can change within a book. So for example, John's gospel is, as its name suggests, a gospel but John 1.1–14 is a piece of poetry; in the same way Colossians is an epistle but Colossians 1.15–20 is also a piece of poetry. We need to bear this in mind as we read because it makes a difference to how we read it.

Also important is translation. Probably the biggest bit of interpretation that happens before anyone even reads the Bible is translation. The words that the translator chooses can shape the way in which we think about a certain text, and being alert to these kinds of issues is important if we are to read the text well. Indeed one of the greatest theological disagreements about the interpretation of the Bible can be traced back to translation and the words with which Gabriel greeted Mary when Gabriel announced Jesus' birth. As we discussed earlier, Roman Catholic translations of the Bible rendered the greeting to Mary as 'Hail Mary, full of grace' implying that Mary was, herself, a vehicle of grace; whereas Protestant translations went for something closer to 'Greetings, favoured one' in which Mary was a recipient of grace but not its vehicle. Small as these kinds of differences may seem, they have significantly changed the face of theological beliefs through the ages.

Another key area is the importance of context. Donald Carson, a famous New Testament scholar, is credited with being the first to say 'a text without a context is a pretext for a proof text'. It has been picked up and used subsequently by many other writers because it is such a good way of making this very important point. What it means is that any verse or saying that is pulled out of its own context in the Bible and used alone can significantly change the meaning of the original text. An example of this is Revelation 3.20 which in the King James Version is

'Behold, I stand at the door, and knock: if any man hear my voice, and open the door, I will come in to him, and will sup with him, and he with me'. This verse has very often been used in evangelistic sermons as the basis of the message of conversion to Christianity. The problem with this is that its context is a letter to the church of Laodicea (the one which is described in Revelation as lukewarm, neither hot nor cold). As a result the verse is aimed at people who are already Christian and reminds them that Jesus stands ready to enter to be with them. The context here changes the verse, even if only a little. What this suggests is that it is vital always to read around any given text to ensure that its context does not change what it might appear to say on the surface.

An extension of this, particularly in books which are telling strong stories, is to pay attention to how the story is told. Often the storytellers have woven together their passage in such a way as to make a point which modern readers often miss because of the way in which they just read one particular part of the Bible (and not the rest around it). Luke's gospel contains some important examples of this. Luke 10.25–37 tells the well-known and well-loved story of the Good Samaritan who stopped to help a stranger in need. What we often miss, however, is the way in which Luke both prepares his readers for this story and then picks up its strands again afterwards.

There are only two mentions of Samaritans in Luke: once in this story and once in the chapter before in Luke 9.52. There the Samaritans would not receive Jesus and his disciples wanted to call down fire on them as punishment. What is clever about this is that, even if Luke's readers did not know of the ancient enmity between Jews and Samaritans (which incidentally is a good example of needing to know historical details that lie behind the text), they would be able to gather that the Samaritans are to be regarded suspiciously simply by having read the chapter before the chapter in which the story of the Good Samaritan occurs. Also important is the story that follows that of the

Good Samaritan. The story of the Good Samaritan ends with the command to 'go and do likewise', the implication being that all Jesus' hearers should, like the Samaritan, care for those along the way. The very next story in Luke is the story of Mary and Martha. In this story Mary sat and listened to Jesus, while Martha was busy with her tasks. Mary is commended for taking time to listen to Jesus. The effect of this is to balance the command to busy oneself with caring. Hearers of Jesus should both care for others *and* take time to stop and listen to his words. One story taken without the other would lead to a lack of balance. The passage in its context reminds us that not only should we not take a verse out of context, we should also not take a passage out of context since doing so will affect how the message is heard.

In front of the text

Probably the most controversial of all the different methods of reading the Bible are in front of the text readings. Many people instinctively still feel that any interpretations of texts should be as objective as possible. They would argue that personal views should be kept as far from interpretations of the text as possible. Others, including myself, would argue that objectivity is impossible. No matter how hard we might try we simply cannot remove our own prejudices or presuppositions from the way in which we read the text. We come to whatever we do shaped by the world in which we live, the experiences that we have had, and the knowledge that we have accumulated. All of this will inevitably affect the way in which we read a text.

At its most simple, an awareness of what is going on in front of the text (i.e. in the mind of the person reading it) is just an exercise in self-awareness and the recognition that who we are will inevitably change the way in which we read the text. So for example, those who read the text from a position of faith will relate to it differently than those who do not; those who tend the land will feel more affinity to agricultural images than those who do not; those who feel oppressed will seek out those passages that speak of freedom with more concentration than those who are not oppressed. The list could go on and on but the point remains. Our lives and circumstances often dramatically affect the way in which we understand things. Simply being aware of this means that we will be more alert to the occasions on which this happens.

Often this kind of interpretation happens without us even being aware of it. I once split a roomful of people into two groups by gender and asked to read and respond to a story in the Old Testament. The story was in Genesis 38 and told the story of Tamar who was married first to one brother and then another but both died. Tamar then dressed as a prostitute and sat on the road that she knew her father-in-law would be travelling by. He, assuming she was a prostitute, slept with her and she became pregnant. The question that we explored was whether Tamar did an understandable thing or not. By and large the women's group thought 'yes' and the men's group 'no'. What this revealed was that, although you can never make hard and fast judgements on these matters, the women had a more natural affinity to the women in the story and the men to the men. Neither groups were aware that they did but it soon became very apparent that this was the case.

One of the real challenges of interpretation of any kind – biblical or not – is that we learn to discover what natural impulses or biases we have which affect the way in which we read a text. We do not necessarily need to change them but simply to be aware that we have them and to notice what difference they make to the conclusions we draw.

In front of the text readings do not stop with simple aware-ness. Many modern interpretations not only become aware of their presuppositions, they deliberately read the text from a cer-tain standpoint. So there are a range of interpretations – as broad a range as the people who are doing this kind of interpretation in fact – which set out to read the Bible from a particular perspective whether it be black, feminist, ecological, post-colonial or something else. These readings pay particular and close attention to the subjectivity that they bring to the text and consciously look for passages or ways of reading the text that respond to this particular standpoint.

The question from which this chapter began was 'does the Bible need interpretation?' The answer, it would seem, is a resounding yes. Not only has it always been interpreted (even the Old Testament interpreted other parts of the Old Testament) but interpretation enhances, enriches and deepens our engagement with the text.

Many modern academic interpretations of the Bible have become so very complex that, often, ordinary readers are overwhelmed or put off by the whole concept of interpretation. What I have tried to show in this chapter, however, is that it is not necessary to abandon the ideas that lie behind interpretation simply because some of the ways in which they are enacted are complex and hard to engage with. The schema that is often cited in interpretation (behind the text, on or in the text, and in front of the text readings) can act as a very helpful aide-mémoire to ensure that all aspects of the text have been explored. If you have asked questions about:

- the history that lies behind the text and how it got into its current form
- the literary form of the text, including its context
- and the presuppositions that you are bringing to the text

then you have probably interpreted the text well.

6
Legacy

In this final chapter, we return to where we began – with the Bible all around us. The vast majority of people do not encounter the Bible in its own pages, since fewer people in Western culture today read the Bible itself than in previous years. Instead they encounter it on the walls of art galleries, in the literature that they read, the music they listen to, and the films they watch. It is here that most people encounter the Bible.

Of course one of the well-documented issues of our age is that, for much of history, people knew their Bibles very well indeed. Therefore you needed to give only the briefest of references or the most general of allusions and people would pick up the biblical reference. The difficulty today is that people do not know the Bible. The Bible may be all around them but people do not notice because they no longer have sufficient knowledge of the Bible to pick up the clues that they see. As a result, there are increasing numbers of books which introduce the Bible for people who are reading English literature so that they can begin to recognize some of the references that it is making to biblical texts, narratives and ideas.

This chapter – like so much else in this book – has to be incredibly selective. Many fine works of art, literature, music and film have had to be ignored not because they are not significant but simply in order to be able to produce a chapter that is vaguely readable and not too long. It does not aim to be in any way exhaustive (and indeed it gets less and less exhaustive as we get closer to the twentieth century when so much more has been painted and written) but to trace major trends and to note some key issues that arise.

The Bible in art

Art in early synagogues and early Christian churches

One of the great challenges for the depiction of the Bible in artwork is, and always has been, the second commandment which forbids the making of idols (Exodus 20.4). This was interpreted as the prohibition of figurative art of any kind, and in Judaism and Christianity of the first few centuries of the Christian era there is, as a result, much less artwork than you might otherwise expect to find. This cautiousness about artwork can also be found reflected in later centuries: indeed there are vigorous condemnations of art in some Medieval Rabbinic texts, and Orthodox Jews today still refrain from any form of figurative art. It is worth noticing, however, that the second commandment is interpreted differently in different communities and Reform and Conservative Jews certainly do have figurative art in their synagogues.

One of the earliest examples of art in a synagogue has been found in a place called Dura-Europos (it is now called Qalat es Salihiye) in the Syrian Desert. Dura-Europos was abandoned suddenly because of a siege of the city but before it was abandoned earth had been piled up against some of the walls to act as protection during the siege. This has led to an extraordinary level of preservation of the frescos on the walls of its buildings. In the synagogue there are a large number of frescos with inscriptions that date to 244–5 AD but there are also traces of earlier figures too. All four walls of the synagogue are covered with paintings including scenes from the life of Moses, the Exodus, Aaron, David, the Ark of the Covenant, Solomon, and even Esther. The purpose of the frescos seems to be to interpret in visual form the key stories of the Bible. The Christian church at Dura-Europos also has images from the Bible from both the Old and the New Testaments.

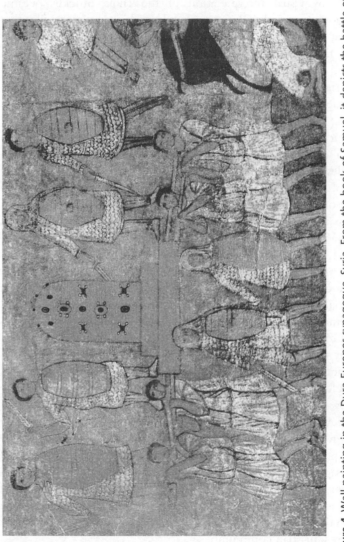

Figure 4 Wall painting in the Dura-Europos synagogue, Syria. From the book of Samuel, it depicts the battle of Eben Ezer where the Ark of the Covenant is taken.

This visual interpretation of the Bible quickly became important in early Christian churches which sought to illustrate what early Christians believed through the artwork decorating the buildings, even before the Scriptures had become a fixed canon. Artwork was often chosen to illustrate the theological significance of Christian belief, and to teach it where reliance on actual texts was not easy. So, for example, in baptistery areas (i.e. places where baptisms took place) there would be extensive depictions of stories connected with water. So the church at Dura-Europos includes many water-inspired themes such as Jesus and Peter walking on the water, the paralytic at the pool of Bethesda, and the woman at the well. Similarly, the importance of the Lord's Supper was depicted with a series of paintings about sacrifice and the sixth-century AD church of San Vitale at Ravenna portrays a range of images which are suggestive of sacrifice.

Artwork appeared not just in buildings dedicated to worship; one of the intriguing features of early Christian art is its use at burials on among other things reliquary caskets where a range of themes that speak of deliverance are used, ranging from Noah's ark to the resurrection of Lazarus. All of these were designed not only to communicate the content of the Bible but to offer ideas about how to interpret what was going on in the Bible. As a result Old Testament passages were linked with those from the New Testament to illustrate the ways in which early Christians believed that the Old Testament pointed to the New. They also suggested how people should think about the key issues of faith. So people could think more deeply about baptism because of passages which used water; about the Lord's Supper due to passages which suggest sacrifice; and death and burial because of passages which talk of deliverance. Artwork very quickly became one of the major ways in which the Bible was interpreted in the early Christian communities.

Art and the Bible in the Byzantine Empire

One of the key periods in Christian art was that of the Byzantine Empire. In 330, the Emperor Constantine moved his capital from Rome to Constantinople (now called Istanbul) and the eastern Roman Empire became known as the Byzantine Empire. Here the imagery both of characters and scenes from the Bible were so significant that they were regarded as having the same importance as the Scriptures did. Byzantine artists believed that art not only depicted the Bible but made its themes present in such a way that could transform the beholder. Byzantine churches were particularly fond of using gold and bright colours in their mosaics which could catch the light and suggest to the worshippers in the church a sense of being in the presence of a glorious mystery. It wasn't just mosaics and frescos that did this but, also, smaller wooden panels, called icons. Icons were believed to be visible expressions of invisible truths, and when they depicted stories from the Bible were believed to be communicating the Bible's message in exactly the same way as the words on the page did.

The extensive influence of art in the Byzantine Empire also gave rise to a period of iconoclasm (the deliberate destruction of public Christian art). One of the greatest occurrences of iconoclasm in the Byzantine Empire took place in the eighth–ninth centuries AD, when hesitations about figurative art in general and depicting the image of Jesus himself in particular reached a climax and caused various public portrayals of him to be destroyed.

Illuminated manuscripts

The illustration of the Bible through art was not restricted to mosaics, frescos and icons – another means of illustration which grew up alongside all of these was the illustration of manuscripts themselves. The earliest example of this is the Quedlinburg Fragment which dates back to the fifth century AD. It contains groups of miniatures (normally between two and five miniatures per page) which lie next to the relevant text. The later illustrated manuscripts, of which the most influential include the St Chad Gospels, the Book of Kells and the Lindisfarne Gospels, contained illustrations both in the text itself as well as on separate pages. As a result accepted ways of depicting each evangelist developed so that even those who could not read the text could recognize who was being depicted:

- Matthew was a man, representing Jesus Christ.
- Mark was a lion, denoting Jesus' triumphal resurrection from the dead.
- Luke was a calf symbolizing Jesus' sacrificial death.
- John was an eagle which suggested Jesus' triumphal second coming.

Again the illustrations were used not just to depict the scenes in the Bible but to suggest the ways in which you might want to understand these passages as a part of Christian faith. Until the fourteenth century, most illuminated manuscripts were produced in monasteries, until demand for them became so great that monasteries began to employ secular illustrators to enable them to complete more manuscripts.

Art and the Bible in the Renaissance and Reformation periods

The Renaissance saw a renewed interest in all things from the ancient world, not least the Bible. One of the big changes that took place in the way in which biblical scenes were depicted was that emotion was increasingly portrayed by artists. Giotto's frescos (1266–1337) at Padua, for example, introduced human

Figure 5 Matthew the Evangelist, Lindisfarne Gospels, *c*.715

feeling into the narratives in a way that Byzantine art did not do. Another shift was an increased interest in the characters and stories of the Bible for their own sake rather than in order to teach something about the spiritual meaning of the story. Donatello's sculptures (*c.*1385–1466) are a good example of this, since here he simply tries to capture the person rather than to try and teach some deeper symbolic meaning. So for example, his sculpture of David does not try to teach anything about the significance of David as a character, it simply depicts him as a boy/man.

Leonardo da Vinci (1452–1519) is widely and popularly acclaimed as one of the greatest artists of this era. Again his work (in paintings like the Last Supper or in the Sistine chapel, or in sculptures like the Pietà or David) his emphasis was on the humanity of the characters portrayed and on the emotion that they might feel, rather than on any more symbolic theological meaning behind the story. Also striking was the fact that artists of this period increasingly set the biblical stories against their own backdrop. The most famous example of this is Dürer (1471–1528) who, using woodcuts, depicted vast numbers of biblical scenes against the backdrop of a contemporary German town.

Dürer's woodcuts were inspired by the writing and teaching of Martin Luther (1483–1546). Luther keenly supported a number of artists in their attempt to depict biblical narratives in this period, among whom L. Cranach the elder (1472–1553) was particularly important since he painted some of the key New Testament narratives, like the death of Jesus, that Luther used to support his doctrine of justification by faith. Not all reformers, however, were as supportive of art as Luther was. Huldrych Zwingli (1484–1531) and John Calvin (1509–64) both returned to the second commandment's prohibition of idols in defence of their insistence on the removal of religious imagery. This removal often degenerated into riots in which statues were smashed and images destroyed. In England, iconoclasm did not affect churches until the civil war in the seventeenth century but then extensive damage was done to buildings, frescos, statues and stained glass windows for similar theological reasons. The civil war and period of the Commonwealth which followed it marked a period of power for the Puritans in Britain. Their religious views led them to attempt to remove as many pieces of artwork from churches as they could in this period.

Art and the Bible in the seventeenth, eighteenth and nineteenth centuries

Following the Reformation, Roman Catholic artists introduced more and more emotion and drama into their depiction of biblical narratives. For example, Caravaggio's paintings (1571–1610) of *The Conversion of St Paul* or the *Supper at Emmaus* take a single dramatic moment in the story as the focus for the picture. In the painting of Paul's conversion Paul has just seen the flash of light and has fallen, blinded, from his horse (indeed Caravaggio is largely responsible for many people imagining a horse at all in this narrative since one is not mentioned in the book of Acts); in the *Supper at Emmaus* the disciples have just recognized who Jesus is and are rising astonished from their seats.

Although from the reformed tradition, Rembrandt (1606–69) was hugely influenced by the Roman Catholic Caravaggio. One of the features of Rembrandt's paintings is not only the drama of Caravaggio but the fact that he depicts his own contemporaries as characters in the narrative. His most famous painting *The Return of the Prodigal Son* is one of his final paintings completed in the last two years of his life. Indeed this painting illustrates much of Rembrandt's approach. Rembrandt painted at least two depictions of the prodigal son, one early in his career when his life was going well and he was at the height of his fame. Then he painted himself as the carousing son who was spending all his inheritance in a far-away land. After a series of personal disasters, Rembrandt died penniless and alone. Before his death, however, he painted the return of the prodigal son in which the son, filled with remorse, begs his father's forgiveness. There is good reason to believe that Rembrandt inserted himself into the story here and read the parable in the light of his own experience.

Figure 6 Rembrandt van Rijn, *The Return of the Prodigal Son*, c.1661–9

As he often did, Rembrandt not only brought the biblical stories to life but inserted the life of his own time into his depiction of the story, even when it was his own troubling autobiography.

In the eighteenth century, William Blake (1757–1857) produced work both in word and picture, not only interpretations of key biblical passages but passionate exhortations about how Christians ought to live. Blake was a mystic, as well as a writer and artist, and his paintings, etchings and writings all depict something of his mystical view of the biblical narrative focusing on angels, God and the heavenly realms.

The Bible continued to be influential in the art of the nineteenth century when some of the most influential artists were the pre-Raphaelite group who, as many artists had before them, depicted biblical narratives against the backdrop of the world in which they lived. A particularly important example of this kind of work is that of William Holman Hunt (1827–1910) whose now iconic depiction of *The Light of the World* gives a powerful interpretation of Jesus standing at the door and knocking in Revelation 3.20; the ground outside the door is full of tangled weeds and is dark and foreboding, presumably illustrating the barren inner landscape of the human soul that Hunt is attempting to depict here. One of the odd features of this painting is that despite the fact that the painting is called *The Light of the World* and that light shines all around Jesus who is knocking at the door, Jesus carries a lamp which as light of the world he should not really need. The second-generation pre-Raphaelites continued the interest in all things classical and biblical and Edward Burne-Jones many times depicted key biblical narratives – particularly those involving angels – using his favourite female models.

Art and the Bible in the twentieth and twenty-first centuries

In the twentieth and twenty-first centuries, depictions of the Bible continue to be produced, though in lower quantities than in previous generations due to fewer commissions. Nevertheless, artists continue to depict the Bible in paintings, sculpture and stained glass (among other media). Many famous artists like Chagall (1887–1985) or Dali (1904–89) used biblical themes for inspiration, and continued to relate these themes to the world in which they painted. In particular, artists in the twentieth and twenty-first centuries often use their portrayal of biblical scenes as a means of protesting against the injustice and inhumanity of the modern world, indeed there have been some powerful modern Pietàs that do just this. A Pietà is a depiction of Mary's grief over her son, Jesus, after his crucifixion. Many modern artists, like Max Ernst, have taken this theme and depicted modern characters in the place of either Mary, or Jesus, or both. Twentieth- and twenty-first-century artists seek, as so many have done before them, to communicate the power and theology of the stories using their own experience and knowledge of the world in which they live.

The Bible in literature

The Bible in literature from the ninth to the fourteenth centuries

The influence of the Bible on English literature really only begins in the seventeenth century once the Bible had been translated into English. Nevertheless it is possible to trace a few examples of the Bible in English literature before then. Probably the earliest examples of the use of the Bible in English literature come from the ninth–tenth centuries and paraphrases of the Bible in manuscripts like the Junius or Caedmon Manuscript which contains paraphrases of part of Genesis, from the creation to Abraham's sacrifice of Isaac, a retelling of the story of the Exodus, and a paraphrase of Daniel (which focused particularly on the fiery furnace). Also significant is the Nowell Codex, from a similar period, which as well as the far more famous *Beowulf* also contains a retelling of the Apocryphal book of Judith.

At this point, the Bible is simply used as a source for paraphrasing but four centuries later it begins to be used more allusively and suggestively as themes are taken from it as the basis of some stories. An example of this is *Sir Gawain and the Green Knight* from the fourteenth century. This story is an extended reflection on salvation, personal responsibility that must be taken for decisions that are made, and forgiveness. There are regular allusions throughout the story both to Adam and Eve and to Christ. In a similar way, the pilgrims in Chaucer's *Canterbury Tales* use the Bible in a variety of ways in their conversations. It is striking that the Bible is assumed to be entirely authoritative and so is used to lend gravitas and authority to what the speaker says. The Bible is quoted as well as alluded to as the means by which moral – or often in the *Tales* immoral – behaviour might be judged.

Once into the fifteenth century it is harder to find evidence of the influence of the Bible on literature, almost certainly because of the prohibition against English language Bibles that grew up following Wycliffe's Bible, but once English translations became popular again from Tyndale in the sixteenth century onwards (see chapter 4, pp. 98–100) then references and allusions to the Bible burgeoned and grew.

The Bible in literature of the sixteenth and seventeenth centuries

Indeed the late sixteenth and early seventeenth century can, in many ways, be seen to be the pinnacle of the Bible's influence on literature. Some of the great writers of this era were steeped deeply in the Bible and this is clearly reflected in their writings. John Donne (1572–1631) is widely acknowledged as one of the greatest metaphysical poets of his generation, and although his early works were largely satires of his contemporary society, later in his life his poetry and then his sermons drew heavily on biblical themes. Two of his most famous quotations – 'No man is an island, entire of itself. Each is a piece of the continent, a part of the main' and 'Therefore, send not to know for whom the bell tolls, it tolls for thee' – both appear in his Meditation 17 from *Devotions Upon Emergent Occasions* (1624). This meditation (part of twenty-three other meditations on recovery from sickness) draws heavily on the biblical concept of humanity's interconnectedness in Christ. Of course, Donne himself continued to influence others so Ernest Hemingway consciously used Donne's quote 'For whom the bell tolls' as the title of his 1940 novel about the Spanish Civil War.

John Donne was a clergyman, as was George Herbert (1593–1633). Herbert's poetry (as well as his proverbs and practical advice for clergy) drew deeply on his spirituality, a spirituality which was shaped by his reading of Scripture. As with Donne, Herbert's poetry demonstrates a deep knowledge of the Bible to which he regularly alludes. For example his poem 'The Altar' which begins 'A broken Altar, Lord thy servant rears, made of a heart, and cemented with teares' is clearly an extended reflection on Psalm 57.17: 'The sacrifice acceptable to God is a broken spirit; a broken and contrite heart, O God, you will not despise.'

In contrast to Donne and Herbert, fellow sixteenth-century authors Christopher Marlowe (1564–93) and William Shakespeare (1564–1616) were not ordained but, nevertheless, drew extensively on the Bible in their plays. Marlowe is thought to make 1037 specific references to the Bible in his plays as well as over 500 more general ones. Shakespeare's plays have even more references to the Bible and there are barely any books of the Bible that are not referred to in his plays, though the books he refers to most often are Job, the Psalms, Sirach, Matthew, Luke and Romans. Shakespeare not only quoted from the Bible but used some of its most important theological ideas as inspiration for his plots. So for example the themes of forgiveness, of human sin and even of kingship can be seen as being drawn from the Bible.

Probably the writer that most people will immediately think of in terms of the Bible's influence on literature is John Milton (1608–74) whose epic poems *Paradise Lost* and *Paradise Regained* evocatively retell the story of the fall of humanity and their expulsion from the Garden of Eden (*Paradise Lost*) and the Temptations of Christ (*Paradise Regained*). The themes of loss and redemption intertwine to make this the powerful work that it is. *Paradise Lost* is often proposed as the finest piece of English literature ever written.

Ten years later another hugely important book was published, which though not as good literature as Milton's poem, may well have had as much, if not more, influence in subsequent generations. John Bunyan's (1628–88) *The Pilgrim's Progress* (whose full title was *The Pilgrim's Progress from This World to That Which Is to Come*) was published in two parts, the first in 1678 and the second in 1684. At one time the *Pilgrim's Progress* was thought to be the most translated and read book after the Bible. It is an allegory about the Christian life and the difficulties that people experience in it which draws heavily on the Bible for its themes.

The Bible in the literature of the eighteenth and nineteenth centuries

The growth of the Enlightenment saw another fall in references to the Bible in English literature, with a few notable exceptions such as *Joseph Andrews*, a novel by Henry Fielding (1707–54) in which the characters draw on the Bible to explain why they act as they do. The late eighteenth and early nineteenth centuries marked another revival in the use of the Bible in literature, though the influence of the Enlightenment can be seen in that the Bible is no longer the sole authoritative source but one among many. William Blake (1758–1827), also an influential artist (see above, p. 153) is a good example of someone whose work is heavily influenced not only by his reading of the Bible but also by Greek mythology and Shakespeare.

Indeed Blake's writing sees a significant development in the use of the Bible in literature, since one of the major strands of his writing is a criticism of the established Church. This use of biblical themes to criticize the Church is one that can be seen in a number of late eighteenth- and nineteenth-century novels. George Eliot's (1819–80) *Silas Marner* presents the book's eponymous hero as someone who loves and is influenced by the Bible but who has rejected the Christianity of his day. The novel itself, in fact, is often seen as being similar in style to the epic narrative of the Old Testament with its themes of trial, retribution and redemption, themes which Eliot paints outside of the Church and not within it. Even more challenging are novels like Thomas Hardy's (1840–1928) *Jude the Obscure* which at times uses the Bible in the opposite way than which it was originally intended. So, for example, Jude is portrayed as being tempted seventy times seven times (II iv 99) a reference to Matthew 18.22 where it is forgiveness not temptation that is described like this.

The Bible in literature of the twentieth century

The novels and poetry of the nineteenth century began to question the previously unquestioned authority of the Bible, a suspicion which in twentieth-century writing reached full bloom. A number of writers of the twentieth century used extensive biblical allusion as a full-blown critique of the Church. So for example W.B. Yeats (1865–1935) returned again and again in his poetry to themes of Christ, the gospels and the second coming and in doing so aimed to show the alien nature of Christian faith and the way in which its influence was waning. This is particularly clear in his poem *The Second Coming* which draws heavily on the book of Revelation which he uses to point towards the ending of the Christian era. T.S. Eliot (1888–1965) was similarly challenging of the Christian Church in that he used extensive biblical allusion throughout his poetry often as part of his critique of the Church. *The Hippopotamus* satires the worldliness of the Church and ends with a quotation from Colossians 4.16 which contains a reference to the Laodiceans. The Laodiceans are the Christian community condemned in Revelation for being luke-warm. Eliot uses the Bible here as a critique of the Church itself and expects his readers to be able to make the connections from the allusions he gives. In a similar way Graham Greene's (1904–91) *The Power and the Glory* features a sinful priest whose humanity leads him into vice and sin and whose character is subtly set against the backdrop of the last supper and Peter's betrayal of Jesus.

Not all twentieth-century literature, however, is so critical of institutional religion. John Steinbeck's (1902–68) *East of Eden* movingly uses Genesis 4 and the story of the rivalry between two brothers as the motivation to tell a profound story of relationship and betrayal. Another much more recent American novel, *Home* by Marilynne Robinson (1943–), uses the story of the prodigal son as inspiration for her re-telling of what happens when the prodigal comes home. By and large American literature continues to use the Bible much more positively that English literature does, though there are exceptions to every rule and it is possible to find examples on either side of the Atlantic which break this rule. Though not high literature, Salley Vickers' novel *Mr Golightly's Holiday* is an example of this. Salley Vickers (1948–) is British and in this story attempts a retelling of the book of Job.

The Bible in music

Music in the Old and New Testaments

Music has always been important in the Bible, particularly in the Old Testament, as a means of expressing faith and worship. The Old Testament writers believed that heaven was populated with angels singing song to God (see for example Job 38.7 which talks about the heavenly beings shouting for joy) and therefore sought to replicate this in their worship in the temple. So important was music in the temple that certain groups of Levites (who were temple servants) were musicians and 1 Chronicles 23.4 makes reference to a four thousand strong choir and orchestra whose job it was to accompany worship in the temple.

This practice of singing continues into New Testament texts and there is extensive evidence that Jesus and the disciples sang ('When they had sung the hymn, they went out to the Mount of Olives', Matthew 26.30) and that the apostle Paul sang ('About midnight Paul and Silas were praying and singing hymns to God, and the prisoners were listening to them', Acts 16.25, and 'I will sing praise with the spirit, but I will sing praise with the mind also', 1 Corinthians 14.15). The early Christians were also encouraged to sing themselves ('as you sing psalms and hymns and spiritual songs among yourselves, singing and making melody to the Lord in your hearts', Ephesians 5.19 and also Colossians 3.16). The question of what Christians sang is harder to answer, since the New Testament never tells us, but it is most likely to be the Psalms of the Old Testament which they would have known well. There are a few poems in the New Testament (like Philippians 2.6–11 and Colossians 1.15–20) which may also have been sung in these early communities.

The Bible and music in the early Church

After the time of the New Testament, the early Christians seem to have continued the practice of singing songs together. Indeed Pliny the Younger refers to them singing a hymn to Christ antiphonally (i.e. first one side would sing and then the other side) though it is assumed that they would have been intoning Psalms. The earliest piece of Christian music comes from the third century AD and was written on the back of a papyrus account for corn in Oxyrynchus in Egypt. It is only a fragment and therefore it is impossible to know exactly what it contained but it is text with music drawing from both the Old and the New Testaments. From what there is there it seems to be calling upon the whole of creation to praise God (Father, Son and Holy Spirit).

At this point the singing may not be what we would recognize as singing and was probably more intoning than singing to a melody. In fact, Clement of Alexandria (150–c.215) banned the use of instruments and the chromatic scale (i.e. the scale with twelve pitches each a semi-tone apart) as being too close to the music of Greek temples. Origen, bishop in Alexandria between c.184 and c.253 AD, even reports that everyone sang in their own mother tongue, suggesting that the singing might have sounded somewhat chaotic.

One of the key developments of early Christian singing can be traced to Arius (who also lived in Alexandria between c.250 and 336), who was subsequently declared to be a heretic because of his views about Christ. Arius set much of his theology to verse which he encouraged people to sing to popular folk songs. This may well be the reason that Athanasius who was a bishop in Alexandria (the same place in which Arius was based) attempted to control the singing of hymns so that the singing was not overly elaborate. Indeed from this grew up an Alexandrian school of singing which was renowned for being severe. Basil of Caesarea (c.329–79) opposed this severe style of music and argued for the importance of a much more melodic style. Ambrose (c.339–97), a bishop in Milan, also contributed to the debate by defining which modes (or scales) were acceptable in church music, and which were not. Even more important than this Ambrose composed numerous hymns which, unusually for the period, were designed to be sung with small groups of notes.

Gregory the Great (c.540–604) nearly two hundred years later imposed new restrictions on singing which changed the nature of church music. Gregory instituted a new mode of chanting in which the voice rose and fell over many notes for one syllable. Eventually four hundred or so years later, and as a result of a number of influences, this chanting became Gregorian chant – attributed to Gregory the Great even if not directly invented by him. Much of what was sung in Gregorian chant came from the Bible and, in particular, established a way of singing the Psalms in a Christian context.

Up until this point, the majority of music was either the singing of actual biblical texts, like the Psalms, or especially written for singing in church contexts.

The Bible and music in the medieval and Reformation periods

Gregorian chant continued to be popular well into the seventeenth–eighteenth centuries but alongside this grew up polyphony which grew out of a harmonization of the chant. Polyphony was regarded by some with severe suspicion because it appeared to introduce secular music into the religious context. Indeed although Pope John XXII (1244–1334) banned polyphony from church music in the fourteenth century, his successor but one, Clement VI (1291–1352), loved it and reintroduced it. Indeed it was in the fourteenth century that the first polyphonic setting of music to be sung in a mass was written, something which subsequently gave rise to the great mass settings of polyphonic composers like Thomas Tallis (1505–85) and William Byrd (1540–1623). In this period, although mass settings became increasingly common, so too were musical settings of biblical passages.

One of the striking features of music at this point is that it had retreated from congregational music and became, instead, the music of professional singers. Martin Luther (1483–1546) sought to return church music to congregations. Luther was a passionate musician and a lute player. He reinstituted congregational hymns and the chorales, as they became known, which were often pre-Reformation hymns translated from Latin into German so that everyone could join in. Luther was concerned, however, to ensure that what was sung contained theology that accorded with that which was preached from the pulpit and as a result wrote numerous hymns that supported his theology.

John Calvin (1509–64), however, who was a leader of the Swiss Reformation, argued only for the singing of Psalms in church since this is what happened in the New Testament; whereas Huldrych Zwingli (1484–1531) who also led the Swiss Reformation opposed any kind of congregational singing at all and often encouraged the smashing of organs to prevent it.

In England the role of music during the Reformation was as varied as the different theological positions held by subsequent monarchs. One of the great issues that arose was that once the Book of Common Prayer was authorized (and insisted upon) for worship, the music that could be sung suddenly diminished almost to nothing since all the previous settings were in Latin. Services in English now needed newly written music and words to accompany them. In 1550 John Merbecke (1510–85) sought to address this issue by setting the Book of Common Prayer to notes (one note per syllable) so that services could once more be set to music. This attempt never really caught on at the time (although it was revived in the nineteenth century and is still used in some Anglican churches today) because during the Elizabethan reign new music began to be composed by fine composers such as Thomas Tallis and John Shepherd (1515–58).

The Bible and music from the Baroque period to the twentieth century

During the period of Oliver Cromwell (1599–1658), the Puritan who ruled as Lord Protector in England between 1653 and 1658, music was banned in churches, which notably included the singing of Christmas carols, but it made a resurgence following the

Restoration with composers such as Henry Purcell (1659–95). Purcell was a Baroque composer, and like many Baroque composers was supported by the Church (Purcell worked at Westminster Abbey) and hence wrote a lot of music which was simply quotations from the Bible set to music.

Also from the Baroque era was the hugely influential Johann Sebastian Bach (1685–1750) who during his lifetime wrote over 1000 different compositions both for voice and for other musical instruments. In terms of his use of the Bible, two of the most important of his pieces are the St Matthew and the St John Passion (he is believed to have written a St Mark and a St Luke Passion as well but these have not survived). Bach's Passions simply tell the story of Jesus' last days and hours directly from the Bible (Matthew and John's gospels respectively) but are interspersed by arias which interpret the text and seek to draw the listener into the story itself. Writing at a similar time to Bach, George Frideric Handel (1685–1759) also used the Bible extensively in his compositions. Alongside the many operas he wrote, Handel also wrote a number of oratorios featuring biblical characters like *Esther*, *Deborah* and *Saul* but of course his most famous of all oratorios is *The Messiah* in which Handel stitched together a remarkable catalogue of Old Testament texts which together communicate the message of who Jesus Christ was. *The Messiah* probably continues to be the most popular piece of music influenced by the Bible ever written.

This putting together of Biblical texts in order to communicate theology continued in works of the classical era. Probably the most famous example from this period was *The Creation* by Franz Joseph Haydn (1732–1809), an Austrian composer. *The Creation* wove together the account of creation from Genesis with words both from the Psalms and from Milton's poem *Paradise Lost*. The text is not thought to have been written by him but nevertheless presents a very interesting interpretation of the stories of creation.

An exploration of music of the classical period must mention the work of Wolfgang Amadeus Mozart (1756–91) who wrote a wide range of incredible music but there is little to say about his work in relation to the Bible. Most of Mozart's sacred works were mass settings – including his famous Requiem – and hence only display the influence of the Bible in as much as the mass itself is heavily influenced by the Bible. He wrote only a very few anthems including a setting of Psalm 46, 'God is our refuge'.

The transition from the classical period to the romantic period of music marks the waning influence of sacred music in general and of the Bible in particular. In the romantic period it was more profitable to write secular music and, since much sacred music had been written at the instigation of powerful patrons in the past, the composition of sacred musical works waned throughout the early nineteenth century. This is illustrated well by Ludwig van Beethoven whose compositions number a little over 200 but who wrote very little sacred music (in all, two masses and an oratorio). Probably his most important work is the oratorio *Christus am Ölberge* (Christ at the Mount of Olives) which imagines the despair that Jesus felt before his crucifixion. One of the key features of it is that it is not simply a quotation of Scripture but an imaginative exercise exploring the grief that Jesus must have felt.

Another key composer in this period was Anton Bruckner (1824–96). While much of the other sacred music composed took the form of mass settings, Bruckner also wrote over thirty motets often using Biblical themes as their basis. The waning of the influence of the Bible on music continued into the twentieth century but, again, this does not mean that there was no biblically inspired music written in this era. A wide range of church commissioned music continued and continues to be written but two composers, in particular, stand out. The first is Francis Poulenc (1899–1963) whose religious reawakening in 1936 gave rise to a number of motets, particularly the Christmas motets which celebrate the birth of Jesus. The other is John Tavener (1944–) whose sacred music draws on biblical themes, though often indirectly through the poetry of William Blake.

The Bible in pop, rock and other music

Of course, classical music is not the only place where the influence of the Bible can be observed. The Bible is also a powerful influence on many different forms of popular contemporary music as well. There are many references to the Bible in contemporary music, though most of these reflect the beliefs of the particular artist and not any kind of commission from churches. Bob Marley (1945–81) was a Jamaican singer-songwriter who was lead singer of the reggae band Bob Marley and the Wailers. Although some of Bob Marley's most famous songs (e.g. *No Woman, No Cry* or *I Shot the Sheriff*) have nothing to do with the Bible, Marley wrote a vast number of songs which drew directly from the Bible. Marley was a Rastafarian, a new religious movement which grew out of Christianity. One of its features was the recognition of the hope that the Bible offered in particular to slaves. Rastafarians therefore used the Bible extensively to understand the world in which they lived. Reggae music drew on this tradition, so much so in fact that it has been described as Bible study in song, and Bob Marley's music illustrates this with songs that reflect on Adam and Eve (*Adam and Eve*, 1975) Genesis 1.26 and the question of whether humanity has dominion over the earth (*We and Dem*, 1980), and freedom (*Exodus*, 1976 and *Redemption Song*, 1980).

Bob Marley's biblical references grew out of his own beliefs. The same is true of Bob Dylan (1941–) who famously became a 'born-again' Christian in the late 1970s and, as a result, produced a number of songs that reflected his Christian faith and which drew from the Bible. Even before that, though, some of his songs drew on biblical texts: *Highway 61 Revisited* (1965) is a fascinating retelling of God's command to sacrifice Isaac (Genesis 22) in which Abraham assumes that God's command must be a joke and God tells Abraham that in future if he sees him coming he'd better run.

At the opposite end of the spectrum Tom Jones' song (1940–) *Delilah* (1968) tells the story of a man who feels betrayed by his girlfriend Delilah. Although not at all close in plot to the story in Judges 13–16, the name Delilah may well be inspired by the story of Samson and Delilah and the name certainly evokes the connotations of a woman who cannot be trusted. Much closer to the biblical narrative is Neil Sedaka's (1939–) *Run Samson Run* (1970) which retells the story of Judges 13–16 from the perspective of a modern love affair and uses it to reflect on the relationship between men and women.

One of the top ten bestselling singles of all time in the UK is the song *Rivers of Babylon* by Boney M. The song was originally a Rastafarian song which was covered by the band in 1978 and takes its lyrics entirely from Psalm 137 (though stopping before the Psalmist expresses the desire to dash the enemies' children against a rock!). This is one of the few songs of its kind to take lyrics entirely from the Bible. Another which does that is *40* by U2 (1983) whose lyrics are taken (as the name suggests) directly from Psalm 40 and are an expression of faith in God. U2 regularly produced songs drawn from Christian faith and the Bible. Another of note is *The First Time* which is a reworking of Luke 15 and the parable of the prodigal son, though with a twist since, when the son returns, he refuses his father's welcome but also notes that once he returned he felt love for the first time.

Leonard Cohen (1934–) is a Jewish singer-songwriter whose religion inspires some of his songs. Probably the best known of all Cohen's songs (because it has been covered over 200 times) is *Hallelujah* (1984), the original version of which contains numerous biblical references including references to the stories of both Samson and Delilah (Judges 13-16) and David and Bathsheba (2 Samuel 11), but before that he produced a number of other songs inspired by biblical texts such as *Story of Isaac* which seeks to make the story of Isaac's sacrifice vivid (and includes details like the colour of Abraham's eyes).

The widespread use of Delilah in rock and pop music draws on the common view of her as an evil woman of no morals. Indeed popular and unflattering pictures of women in the Bible are regularly picked up in various ways. It is therefore striking to notice Sade's (1959–) song *Jezebel* (1985) which refutes the popular view of King Ahab's wife and instead portrays her as a strong, confident and determined woman who should be admired and not despised.

Bruce Cockburn (1945–) is a Canadian folk/rock singer who has been in bands since the 1960s. His 1990 song *Cry of a Tiny Babe* is the re-telling of Matthew's birth narrative of Jesus and reflects on the importance of Jesus' birth, noting, in particular, the significance of the Redemption that he brought. The Grateful Dead also began their careers in the 1960s and produced a number of songs based on biblical narratives. *Samson and Delilah* (1977) takes the well-used theme of Judges 13–16 and again, as so often, paints Delilah in an almost entirely negative light. Meanwhile their 1987 song *My Brother Esau* uses the story of the two warring brothers to reflect on the Vietnam War.

Another more unusual biblical passage lies behind Kate Bush's (1958–) song *Song of Solomon* which as its name suggests draws lines from the biblical book (also known as the Song of Songs) to plead with her lover for love and solace. This song uses the lines from the Song of Solomon to reflect on what it felt like to be in love and to yearn for someone else.

In the Crash Test Dummies song *God Shuffled his Feet* (1993) the song describes God preparing a feast of bread and wine for people (a clear reference to the Christian Eucharist) and while they eat the food people ask God all sorts of questions about what heaven is like and whether you need a haircut in heaven.

There are all sorts of other songs one could list as evidence of the influence of the Bible in pop and rock music but time and space prevent this. Nevertheless, a good place to end this exploration is with Bruce Springsteen (1949–) and his 2005 song *Jesus was an Only Son* which imagines the final conversation between Mary and Jesus before Jesus died. Springsteen uses evocative language to emphasize the pain and suffering for both Jesus and Mary involved in Jesus' death.

The Bible in film

Last, but by no means least, is the way in which film uses the Bible. Although there would be some grounds for arguing that film fits alongside art, in reality it is a combination of art, literature and music and therefore fits best at the end of a chapter that has just explored these other three. Film is the most recent of all artistic expressions and is only just over 100 years old. Nevertheless in this short period the influence of the Bible on film has waxed and waned significantly. It is hardly surprising to note that many fewer films today are made on biblical themes than fifty to sixty years ago. What is intriguing, however, is that at the end of the 1950s six out of the ten most popular films of that decade were biblical epics.

Biblical epics

Samson and Delilah (1949) was hugely popular as a film and for the most part simply retold the narrative from Judges. One of the main ways in which it departed from the text is that it portrayed Delilah (played by Hedy Lamarr to Victor Mature's Samson) as falling deeply in love with Samson and feeling subsequent remorse for her betrayal of him, so much so that she refused to leave him when, at the end, he destroyed the temple of Dagon and died with him in the ruins. This interpretation has had lasting impact on the popular imaginings of this story and may go some way towards explaining why the story was such a popular subject for contemporary music, particularly in the 1960s and 1970s.

Two years later an epic of a different kind was produced, *Quo Vadis* (1951). This was not strictly speaking a biblical epic since it was set in Rome between 64 and 68 AD and features the conflict then between Nero and the Christian community. Behind it, however, lurks the shadow of the New Testament, not least at the end when Peter's crook sprouted flowers and in the background the saying from John's gospel 'I am the way, the truth and the life' is intoned. Also in that year, *David and Bathsheba* was brought out (starring Gregory Peck and Susan Hayward). In many ways it was a similar kind of film to *Samson and Delilah*, telling, as a love story, one of the great narratives of the Old Testament (found in 2 Samuel 11).

Following that, in 1953 another film, *The Robe*, came out. *The Robe* was a little more like *Quo Vadis* in style since it was set in the Roman era and followed a (fictional) Roman tribune by the name of Marcellus Gallio (played by Richard Burton) whose unit crucified Jesus and who was subsequently tormented by remorse for what he had done. The story carries on from there to follow Marcellus who becomes a missionary alongside Paul and is eventually condemned to death (along with his childhood sweetheart Diana, played by Jean Simmons) for his defiance of Caligula.

In 1956, the film world returned to the Old Testament with the grand epic *The Ten Commandments* starring Charlton Heston and Yul Brynner, as Moses and Pharaoh respectively. This is the first Old Testament epic based not on a love story but simply on the narrative of Moses' freeing of the people of God from Egypt. It takes in the whole of Moses' life, from birth to death, and by and large simply tells the story of Moses' life. The film that epitomizes the 1950s glory days of biblical epics is *Ben Hur* (1959), again starring Charlton Heston. In a similar way to *Quo Vadis* and

The Robe, Ben Hur takes the New Testament narrative sideways on, and contains a string of encounters with Jesus which culminate in Jesus' death and Ben Hur's recognition of who he really was.

Films about Jesus

The 1950s may have been the high spot of the popularity of biblical epics but the influence of the Bible on film remained. Following the 1950s, more films focusing specifically on Jesus' life were made. These differed from *The Robe* and *Ben Hur* in that Jesus played the starring role (and spoke, unlike in the previous films). The first of these films was called *King of Kings* (1961), and starred Jeffrey Hunter. It portrayed Jesus as a non-political character against a much more political Barabbas who sought to overthrow the Roman Empire. The film was not well received critically and unlike its biblical epic predecessors from the 1950s made a significant loss at the box office.

The makers of *The Greatest Story Ever Told* were not put off by this and four years later produced another film about Jesus' life (1965). They cast an unknown actor in the role of Jesus but had many famous stars in cameo roles (not least John Wayne as the Roman centurion who declared, at Jesus' death, that he was the son of God). Although some considered it powerful and moving, the film was not a success (and is estimated to have made only about seventeen per cent of what it needed to break even), and dissuaded the Hollywood film industry from attempting other biblical epics of this scale for quite some time.

Just before this, in Italy, however, another film was made by an Italian director called Pier Paolo Pasolini. He based his film on just one gospel (hence its name *The Gospel According to St Matthew*) and used an unprofessional cast as actors. It is widely regarded as a beautifully shot film which builds its atmosphere by camera angle and cleverly chosen music, rather than big budget effects.

The 1970s saw a new era of films and in particular in 1973 two musicals based on his life. The first, *Jesus Christ Superstar*, by Tim Rice and Andrew Lloyd Webber, retold the last week of Jesus' life using ancient sets but modern weaponry and costume (except for Jesus who wore a more usual white robe). Also in the same year *Godspell* was made into a film. The only features that tie it to *Jesus Christ Superstar* are that it was produced in the same year and that it was also a musical. In other ways it is very different and tells the story of Jesus through a series of Jesus' parables interspersed with songs which are largely the lyrics of traditional hymns set to modern tunes.

JOSEPH AND THE AMAZING TECHNICOLOR DREAMCOAT

Probably one of the best-loved biblical musicals of all time is *Joseph and the Amazing Technicolor Dreamcoat*. Although written before *Jesus Christ Superstar*, *Joseph* only began to be performed in full after the success of *Jesus Christ Superstar*. The show appeared in the West End in 1973 and on Broadway in 1982. It has been recorded as an album starring various singers and also made into a DVD starring Donny Osmond (1999).

Alongside its professional success, the show is well loved by schools and it is estimated that it has been put on in schools over 20,000 times. *Joseph* has an almost entirely sung script, with very little narrative at all, and the catchy, easy-to-sing songs are what has contributed to its popularity.

Many biblical scholars would describe the Joseph story as a 'novella' with clear characterization, plot progression, and even some, failed, romance. It is probably the focused nature of the story combined with the strands of a dysfunctional family, false sexual accusation, and the rise of the hero from poverty to power that have made this story so abidingly popular – and hence so easy to turn into a musical like *Joseph*.

> The show remains successful and popular over forty years after it was first written and has received numerous awards both for its original production and for its subsequent revivals.

The next film about Jesus was made not for the big screen but for television (since it ran for over six hours). Made by Franco Zeffirelli, *Jesus of Nazareth* starred Robert Powell (with strikingly blue eyes) and was designed to be a reverential and thoughtful retelling not just of the story of Jesus but of the emotions felt by those around him. Two years later a film of a very different kind caused great controversy. The *Life of Brian* (1979) produced by Monty Python is not, in fact, a life of Jesus at all. Instead it is an entirely fictional narrative set in first-century Jerusalem which sought to satirize Christian sentimentality and over-earnestness. The film has been highly influential in popular culture and lines such as 'Blessed are the cheese makers' and 'he's not the Messiah, he's a very naughty boy' have passed into modern parlance.

Even more controversial was the 1988 film, *The Last Temptation of Christ* by Martin Scorsese which portrays a Jesus who is deeply reluctant to fulfil his calling and is, ultimately, saved from death by his guardian angel so that he can marry Mary Magdalene and live a normal and happy life. This film caused more outrage than any other – largely because it departed more from the biblical narrative than any other life of Jesus had before it. The following year, another film, *Jesus of Montreal* (1989), which was French Canadian, also caused a small amount of controversy since it portrayed a small acting company who put on a passion play only to find the story of Jesus taking over their lives. In the end the character that played Jesus was killed and his body gave new life to numerous people through organ donation.

The most recent film about Jesus was Mel Gibson's *The Passion of the Christ* (2004) which stunned the film-making world by being a box office success. It focuses on the last twelve hours of Jesus' life, is deeply and horrifically violent at times, and has a dialogue entirely in Hebrew, Aramaic or Latin, with subtitles. Nevertheless, the film is widely applauded for being powerfully and beautifully shot. Critics are split over whether the violence mars the overall message of the film.

The Bible in cartoon

Although these are the most influential of films, it would be wrong to stop an exploration of the Bible in film without mention of a few significant cartoons. One of the most successful biblical cartoons was *The Prince of Egypt* (1998) by Dreamworks animation which provides a retelling of the story of Moses, with songs by Stephen Schwartz. It was enormously popular and when it was brought out grossed more at the box office than any film had done before it. Its sequel (or more accurately prequel) featured a retelling of the story of Joseph (*Joseph: King of Dreams*, 2000) but it was much less popular and was brought out straight to video.

The other film-length animation of note is *The Miracle Maker* (2000), a mixture of stop animation and cartoon, which retells the story of the gospels from the perspective of Jairus' daughter (who in the film is called Tamar).

This glance through the influence of the Bible in art, literature, music and film demonstrates powerfully the influence of the Bible on the culture all around us. It is clear that, in some areas at least, influence is waning as fewer pieces of art or pieces of classical music are commissioned. Nevertheless, the Bible continues to be influential both in a number of modern works (noticeably music and film) and in the vast body of art, literature and music which has been handed down to us by previous generations.

The Bible is truly all around us and our pictures of the narratives it tells are irrevocably shaped by these cultural interpretations. So, for example, many people imagine Paul on a horse on

Figure 7 Moses, in the Dreamworks feature-length cartoon, *The Prince of Egypt*

the road to Damascus largely because of Caravaggio's painting; or Delilah in love with Samson due to the 1949 biblical epic film about them. Even if we haven't seen either that painting or that film, the depiction has seeped into modern consciousness and shapes the way many people think and feel about key narratives.

At the same time, while we can pick up a lot of our knowledge about the Bible from art, literature, music and film, big gaps occur if we rely solely on those media for our knowledge (in other words we would know the story of Samson and Delilah very well indeed but other parts of the Bible, like the book of Ruth, much less well). Another problem, particularly for the art and literature which comes from earlier generations, is that the artists and authors from times past assumed that their audiences knew the Bible. As a result they did not explain the allusions or images that they made. Without a rudimentary knowledge of the Bible many references can feel obscure and impossible to understand.

The Bible is all around us and continues to influence the world in which we live. This book has sought to offer a brief glimpse not only of its contents but also of the long journey it has taken to reach the form it is in today and of the impact it has made and continues to make on the world in which we live.

Further reading

If you would like to read further on this subject then a selection of books are given below, ordered to correspond with the chapters of this book.

Introduction

If you are hoping for a how to read the Bible guide then there are numerous books available, from Gordon D. Fee and Douglas Stuart, *How to Read the Bible Book by Book: A Guided Tour* (Zondervan, 2002) and *How to Read the Bible for All Its Worth* (new edn, Zondervan, 2003) to Richard Holloway, *How to Read the Bible* (Granta Books, 2006) (these books present very different ways of reading the Bible).

History

Many introductions to the Old and New Testaments tell the story of the Bible in more detail than it was possible to do here. Some of the most popular of these introductions include John Drane, *Introducing the Old Testament* (3rd edn, Lion Hudson Plc, 2011), or for the Old Testament alone B. Anderson, *The Living World of the Old Testament* (4th edn, Longman, 1988). These remain reliable guides. Also helpful to gain an overview of history is Pat Alexander and David Alexander, *The Lion Handbook to the Bible* (4th edn, Lion Hudson Plc, 2009).

For those who would prefer a slightly more conservative introduction to the Old and New Testaments the volumes by Tremper Longman III and Raymond B. Dillard (eds), *An Introduction to the Old Testament* (Apollos, 2007) and D.A. Carson and Douglas J. Moo, *An Introduction to the New Testament* (2nd edn, Apollos, 2005) are both very good. For something more in depth and scholarly two reliable and inspiring introductions are Walter Brueggemann, *An Introduction to the Old Testament: The Canon and Christian Imagination* (Westminster/John Knox Press, 2004) and David A. deSilva, *An Introduction to the New Testament: Contexts, Methods and Ministry Formation* (illustrated edn, IVP, 2004).

There are endless books that explore the archaeology of the events in the Bible and which set out varying claims for its historicity. A good introduction to the current state of affairs can be found in Eric H. Cline, *Biblical Archaeology: A Very Short Introduction* (OUP USA, 2009). Those who want to explore more detail on some of the differing positions might enjoy William G. Dever, *What Did the Biblical Writers Know* (William B. Eerdmans Publishing Co., 2003) which maintains what some have called a maximalist view of history, and Philip R. Davies, *In Search of Ancient Israel* (2nd edn, Sheffield Academic Press, 1995) which presents an opposing view.

For people who wish to follow up the history in more detail some of the best books are J. Maxwell Miller and John H. Hayes, *History of Ancient Israel and Judah* (2nd edn, SCM Press, 2006) and Lester L. Grabbe, *Introduction to Second Temple Judaism: History and Religion of the Jews in the Time of Nehemiah, the Maccabees, Hillel and Jesus* (T. & T. Clark Ltd, 2010).

Genre

For more on reading the books of the Bible as they are ordered in the Hebrew Scriptures see Marvin A. Sweeney, *Tanak:*

A Theological and Critical Introduction to the Jewish Bible (Fortress Press, 2011) which explores the importance of the Hebrew Scriptures themselves in the order in which they are found in Hebrew.

For more on reading the Bible as literature see Gordon D. Fee and Douglas Stuart, *How to Read the Bible for All Its Worth* (new edn, Zondervan, 2003); Steven L. McKenzie, *How to Read the Bible: History, Prophecy, Literature – Why Modern Readers Need to Know the Difference and What It Means for Faith Today* (OUP USA, 2009); and Leland Ryken, *How to Read the Bible as Literature … and Get More Out of It* (Zondervan, 1984).

There has, of course, been much written on the different types of genre within the Bible. For more on each particular style of writing see the following.

On Law: T. Desmond Alexander, *From Paradise to the Promised Land: An Introduction to the Pentateuch* (3rd edn, Baker Academic, 2012); Paula Gooder, *Pentateuch: A Story of Beginnings* (reprint, T. & T. Clark Ltd, 2004); and James W. Watts, *Reading Law: The Rhetorical Shaping of the Pentateuch* (1st edn, Continuum International Publishing, 1999).

On the historical books: Victor P. Hamilton, *Handbook on the Historical Books: Joshua, Judges, Ruth, Samuel, Kings, Chronicles, Ezra-Nehemiah, Esther* (illustrated edn, Revell, a division of Baker Publishing Group, 2001); David M. Howard Jr., *An Introduction to the Old Testament Historical Books* (Moody Press, 2007); and Steven L. McKenzie, *Introduction to the Historical Books: Strategies for Reading* (William B. Eerdmans Publishing Co., 2010).

On the Psalms: Walter Brueggemann, *The Psalms and the Life of Faith* (Augsburg Fortress, 1995); John Eaton, *Psalms for Life* (SPCK Publishing, 2006); and Jonathan Magonet, *A Rabbi Reads the Psalms* (2nd rev. edn, SCM Press, 2004).

On the Prophets: Robert B. Chisholm, *Handbook on the Prophets* (Baker Academic, 2009); Jack R. Lundbom, *The Hebrew Prophets: An Introduction* (Augsburg Fortress, 2010); John Millar,

Meet the Prophets: Beginner's Guide to the Books of the Biblical Prophets (Paulist Press International, 1987); and John F. A. Sawyer, *Prophecy and the Biblical Prophets* (2nd rev. edn, OUP Oxford, 1993).

On wisdom literature: Roland E. Murphy, *The Tree of Life: An Exploration of Biblical Wisdom Literature* (3rd edn, William B. Eerdmans Publishing Co., 2002); Alastair Hunter, *Wisdom Literature* (SCM Press, 2006); and Craig Bartholomew and Ryan P. O'Dowd, *Old Testament Wisdom Literature* (Apollos, 2011).

On apocalyptic literature in general: John J. Collins, *The Apocalyptic Imagination: An Introduction to the Jewish Apocalyptic Literature* (2nd rev. edn, William B. Eerdmans Publishing Co., 1998); Christopher Rowland, *The Open Heaven: A Study of Apocalyptic in Judaism and Early Christianity* (Wipf & Stock Publishers, 2002); and D.S. Russell, *Divine Disclosure: Introduction to Jewish Apocalyptic* (1st edn, SCM Press, 1992); and on Revelation in particular see Ian Boxall, *Revelation: Vision and Insight: Vision and Insight – An Introduction to the Apocalypse* (SPCK Publishing, 2002) and Simon Woodman, *The Book of Revelation* (illustrated edn, SCM Press, 2008).

On the gospels: Richard Bauckham, *Jesus and the Eyewitnesses: The Gospels as Eyewitness Testimony* (William B. Eerdmans Publishing Co., 2008); Richard A. Burridge, *What are the Gospels?* (Eerdmans 2004); Richard A. Burridge, *Four Gospels, One Jesus?* (Classic edn, SPCK Publishing, 2013); James D.G. Dunn, *Jesus Remembered: Christianity in the Making* (vol. 1, William B. Eerdmans Publishing Co., 2003); Graham Stanton, *The Gospels and Jesus* (2nd edn, OUP Oxford, 2002); and N.T. Wright, *Jesus and the Victory of God: Christian Origins and the Question of God* (vol. 2, SPCK Publishing, 1996).

On Paul's epistles: Morna D. Hooker, *Paul: A Beginner's Guide* (Oneworld Publications, 2008); Jerome Murphy-O'Connor, *Paul: His Story* (new edn, OUP Oxford, 2005); E.P. Sanders, *Paul: A Very Short Introduction* (new edn, OUP Oxford, 2001); and Tom Wright, *What Saint Paul Really Said* (Lion Hudson Plc, 1997);

and on the Catholic epistles Andrew Chester and Ralph P. Martin, *The Theology of the Letters of James, Peter, and Jude* (Cambridge University Press, 1994) and Darian Lockett, *An Introduction to the Catholic Epistles* (T. & T. Clark Ltd, 2011).

Canon

There are a number of books available on the formation of the canon of Scripture. For good general overviews of the subject see John Barton, *How the Bible Came to Be* (Darton, Longman and Todd, 1997) or for a longer treatment of the subject F.F. Bruce, *The Canon of Scripture* (new edn, IVP USA, 1988) which argues for an earlier closing of the canon, or Lee Martin McDonald, *The Biblical Canon: Its Origin, Transmission, and Authority* (Baker Academic, 2007) which argues for a later closing of the canon. Also interesting is Lee Martin McDonald and James A Sanders (eds), *The Canon Debate* (Baker Academic, 2001). In terms of the New Testament canon alone probably the best book on the subject is Bruce M. Metzger, *The Canon of the New Testament: Its Origin, Development, and Significance* (new edn, Clarendon Press, 1997).

For those whose Bible does not contain a copy of the Apocrypha it is possible to buy these separately in different versions, particularly in the new Revised Standard Version. The easiest and more reliable way to access the texts in the Old Testament pseudepigrapha is in James H. Charlesworth (ed.), *The Old Testament Pseudepigrapha* (vols 1 & 2, Hendrickson Publishers Inc, 2010) and the New Testament Apocrypha can be found either in J.K. Elliott (ed.) *The Apocryphal New Testament: A Collection of Apocryphal Christian Literature in an English Translation* (OUP Oxford, 2005) or in W. Schneemelcher, *New Testament Apocrypha* (vols 1 & 2, Westminster/John Knox Press, 2006).

There are a number of introductions to these collections. Some of the best include the following.

On the Septuagint and its importance, Jennifer Dines, *The Septuagint* (Continuum International Publishing, 2004); and Karen H. Jobes and Silva Moises, *Invitation to the Septuagint* (Baker Academic, 2005) are good introductions.

On the Old Testament pseudepigrapha the best thing to do is to look for a guide on a particular book. The Sheffield Academic Press guides to the Apocrypha and pseudepigrapha provide helpful introductions to all the key books in the pseudepigrapha.

On the New Testament Apocrypha one of the best ways in is with Fred Lapham, *Introduction to the New Testament Apocrypha* (Continuum Publishing Corporation, 2003).

Many books have been written on the issue of the authority of Scripture, so many in fact, it is impossible to do them all justice. For a helpful book that contains a wide range of views try William P. Brown (ed.), *Engaging Biblical Authority: Perspectives on the Bible as Scripture* (Westminster/John Knox Press, 2007). A well-written book which explores the doctrine of inerrancy in a more modern perspective is Kenton L. Sparks, *God's Word in Human Words: An Evangelical Appropriation of Critical Biblical Scholarship* (Baker Academic, 2008). Finally two smaller more introductory books worth reading are John Barton, *People of the Book?: The Authority of the Bible in Christianity* (3rd rev. edn, SPCK Publishing, 2011) and Tom Wright, *Scripture and the Authority of God* (SPCK Publishing, 2005).

Translation

Two useful introductions to the Targums are John Bowker, *The Targums & Rabbinic Literature: An Introduction to Jewish Interpretations of Scripture* (Cambridge University Press, 2009) and Paul

Virgil McCracken Flesher and Bruce Chilton, *Targums: A Critical Introduction* (Baylor University Press, 2011), though readers should know that although these are both introductions, they are certainly not basic introductions.

As noted in the previous chapter, two of the best introductions to the Septuagint are Jennifer Dines, *The Septuagint* (Continuum International Publishing, 2004) and Karen H. Jobes and Silva Moises, *Invitation to the Septuagint* (Baker Academic, 2005).

A very good brief introduction to the texts of the New Testament remains F.F. Bruce, *The New Testament Documents: Are They Reliable?* (William B. Eerdmans Publishing Co., 2003), but for something much more comprehensive see Bruce M. Metzger and Bart D. Ehrman, *The Text of the New Testament: Its Transmission, Corruption, and Restoration* (4th edn, OUP USA, 2005).

Again Metzger provides one of the most thorough and helpful overviews of Bible translation in Bruce M. Metzger, *Bible in Translation: Ancient and English Versions* (Baker Publishing Group, 2001). There exist some fascinating studies of individual translators and translations including: G.R. Evans, *John Wyclif: A Biography* (Lion Hudson Plc, 2007) and David Daniell, *William Tyndale: A Biography* (new edn, Yale University Press, 2001). There are endless books on the King James Version especially following its 400th anniversary; some of the best of these include: Melvyn Bragg, *The Book of Books: The Radical Impact of the King James Bible 1611–2011* (Hodder & Stoughton, 2011); Gordon Campbell, *Bible: The Story of the King James Version* (OUP Oxford, 2011); and Adam Nicolson, *When God Spoke English: The Making of the King James Bible* (HarperPress, 2011).

Two other good books on Bible translation and translations are Glen G. Scorgie, Mark L. Strauss and Steven M. Voth (eds), *The Challenge of Bible Translation: Communicating God's Word to the World* (Zondervan, 2003) and Gordon D. Fee and Mark L. Strauss,

How to Choose a Translation for All Its Worth: A Guide to Understanding and Using Bible Versions (Zondervan, 2007).

Interpretation

There are extensive books written on the interpretation of the Bible.

The exploration of the way in which the New Testament writers used the Old Testament is a rapidly growing area. Two good introductions to the field are Steve Moyise, *Old Testament in the New Testament* (T. & T. Clark International, 2004) and Stanley E. Porter (ed.), *Hearing the Old Testament Through the New Testament* (William B. Eerdmans Publishing Co., 2006).

To understand Jewish interpretation of the Bible better you can either look at ancient interpretations alone for which see John Bowker, *The Targums & Rabbinic Literature: An Introduction to Jewish Interpretations of Scripture* (Cambridge University Press, 2009) or ancient and modern interpretations for which Karin Hedner Zetterholm, *Jewish Interpretation of the Bible: Ancient and Contemporary* (Fortress Press, 2012) offers a good guide.

Each period of Christian interpretation has extensive literature written about it. A very helpful series is Alan J. Hauser and Duane F. Watson (eds), *A History of Biblical Interpretation* (William B. Eerdmans Publishing Co., 2009) which in multiple volumes traces the major themes of Biblical interpretation through history.

For more specific introductions to each period, see:

- F. Karlfried, *Biblical Interpretation in the Early Church* (Augsburg Fortress, 1985).
- Susan Boynton and Diane Reilly, *The Practice of the Bible in the Middle Ages: Production, Reception and Performance in Western Christianity* (Columbia University Press, 2011).

- Richard A. Muller and John L. Thompson (eds), *Biblical Interpretation in the Era of the Reformation* (William B. Eerdmans Publishing Co., 1997).
- Jonathan Sheehan, *The Enlightenment Bible: Translation, Scholarship, Culture* (new edn, Princeton University Press, 2007).

On the subject of biblical interpretation in general some of the most helpful books include:

- John Barton (ed.), *The Cambridge Companion to Biblical Interpretation* (Cambridge University Press, 1998).
- Paula Gooder, *Searching for Meaning: An Introduction to Interpreting the New Testament* (SPCK Publishing, 2008).
- David Holgate and Rachel Starr, *Biblical Hermeneutics* (SCM Press, 2006).
- W.R. Tate, *Biblical Interpretation: An Integrated Approach* (3rd edn, Baker Academic, 2008).

Those who would like books to fill in elements of historical background to the text will enjoy Kenneth E. Bailey, *Jesus Through Middle Eastern Eyes: Cultural Studies in the Gospels* (SPCK Publishing, 2008) and *Paul Through Mediterranean Eyes: Cultural Studies in 1 Corinthians* (SPCK Publishing, 2011); also John Drane, *Introducing the Old Testament* (3rd, colour edn, Lion Hudson Plc, 2011) and *Introducing the New Testament* (3rd, rev. colour edn, Lion Hudson Plc, 2010).

Legacy

Two books that are relevant to the whole of this chapter are Maggi Dawn, *The Writing on the Wall: High Art, Popular Culture and the Bible* (Hodder & Stoughton, 2012) and Dee Dyas and Esther Hughes, *The Bible in Western Culture: The Student's Guide*

(Routledge, 2005). Both of these seek to be introductions to the way in which the Bible has been used in culture; both go through the Bible in order noting the key themes and how they are used in art, literature and music.

For those interested in the influence of the Bible in art both John Drury, *Painting the Word: Christian Pictures and Their Meanings* (new edn, Yale University Press, 2002) and Jeffrey Spier, Herbert L. Kessler, et al., *Picturing the Bible: The Earliest Christian Art* (Yale University Press, 2009) are very good. A more technical, but nevertheless fascinating book is J. Cheryl Exum and Ela Nutu (eds), *Between the Text and the Canvas: The Bible and Art in Dialogue* (Sheffield Phoenix Press, 2007).

In the field of the Bible and literature an enormously helpful resource is David Jasper and Stephen Prickett (eds), *The Bible and Literature: A Reader* (Wiley-Blackwell, 1999); this places passages from the Bible next to relevant passages of literature and illustrates the different ways in which the Bible is used in literary texts. Also helpful is Alison Jack, *The Bible and Literature* (SCM Press, 2012), which is an introduction to the whole area.

In music and the Bible the field is so vast that it is best to look at some of the more specific books either on particular singers, like Michael J. Gilmour, *Tangled Up in the Bible: Bob Dylan and Scripture* (illustrated edn, Continuum International Publishing Group Ltd, 2004) and *Call Me the Seeker: Listening to Religion and Popular Music* (Continuum, 2005), or on particular parts of the Bible, like Dan W. Clanton, *Daring, Disreputable and Devout: Interpreting the Hebrew Bible's Women in the Arts and Music* (T. & T. Clark Ltd, 2009); Mark McEntire and Joel Emerson, *Raising Cain, Fleeing Egypt and Fighting Philistines: The Old Testament and Popular Music* (Smyth & Helwys, 2007); Samuel L. Terrien, *The Magnificat: Musicians as Biblical Interpreters* (Paulist Press International, 1994); Helen Leneman, *Love, Lust, and Lunacy: The Stories of Saul and David in Music* (Sheffield Phoenix Press, 2010) and *The Performed Bible: The Story of Ruth in Opera and Oratorio* (Sheffield Phoenix Press, 2007).

Writing about the Bible and film is a growing subject and there are numerous books which are helpful; some of my own favourites are Bruce Francis Babington and Peter William Evans, *Biblical Epics: Sacred Narrative in the Hollywood Cinema* (Wipf & Stock Publishers, 2009); W. Barnes Tatum, *Jesus at the Movies: A Guide to the First Hundred Years* (rev. edn, Polebridge Press, 2000); L. Joseph Kreitzer, *Gospel Images in Fiction and Film: On Reversing the Hermeneutical Flow* (Continuum International Publishing Group Ltd, 2002); and *Pauline Images in Fiction and Film: On Reversing the Hermeneutical Flow* (Continuum International Publishing Group, 1999).

Biblical index

General index